FOREWORD

Having been associated with the Citizens Advice Service over many years, I know from first hand experience that one of the most common but also the most traumatic of problems to be brought to advice agencies such as CAB, are those connected with separation and divorce. For clients it is a time of great stress when clear, lucid and comprehensible advice is a necessity. I am delighted, therefore, to welcome the publication of this new edition of Splitting Up, and to provide this foreword.

Dr Nichols has once again succeeded in producing a plain English guide to tackling the mass of real -life problems associated with the breakdown of long term relationships. His industry and commitment to the provision of helpful, practical advice is much to be commended.

Professor Alan Paterson Chair, Citizens Advice Scotland Legal Services Group.

The information in this book is based on the law as at May 1998. You should check whether changes have occurred, especially in the various sums of money mentioned. While the intention in this book is to be as comprehensive as possible, splitting up can be a complex and difficult area on which to give advice. You are recommended to use this as a good general introduction but before taking any action, to seek advice from a Citizens Advice Bureau, professional advisor or solicitor about your individual situation.

CONTENTS

CONTENTS cont...

CHAPTER ONE

INTRODUCTION
THINKING THINGS OVER

Organisations which can help

Citizens Advice Bureaux
Marriage counsellors
Family Mediation Scotland
CALM
Women's Aid
Shelter
One Parent Families Scotland
Housing departments
Housing associations
Benefits Agency
Child Support Agency
Gingerbread
Other sources of help

Solicitors

Do I need a solicitor?

Legal aid

This book is about splitting up – you and your partner separating or getting divorced. It is a very stressful experience with serious emotional and financial consequences. Not only have you to adjust to living without your former partner, but there are a host of practical matters which you will have to think about – such as where to stay, who is to look after the children, how to get enough money to live on, how splitting up will affect your tax and social security position. These are dealt with in detail in the following chapters.

It is worthwhile thinking about all of these things before you decide to leave your partner because once the process of splitting up has started it is very difficult to stop it. Don't rush into making a decision you might later regret.

Many problems in a relationship are due to a lack of communication between partners or a misunderstanding of the other's needs and desires. You may find that talking things over with your partner or consulting one of the organisations listed below resolves the problems between you. On the other hand, your relationship may have deteriorated to such an extent that reconciliation is impossible and splitting up is the only sensible answer. Even in this case talking things over with your partner may help in arriving at mutually agreeable solutions to the problems each of you will face in the future.

A free specialist service is available for couples who have decided to split up and want help to make arrangements for the children. A mediator can work with you and your partner to reach an agreement about the children. This type of assistance can help you to avoid painful and lengthy court battles. The mediator does not take sides or try to get you to stay together. If through talking with the mediator it seemed that there was some chance of you and your partner being able to stay together you would be encouraged to go to another agency.

See p7–11 for addresses of the mediation service and other agencies.

Think about consulting your (and perhaps even your partner's) family before making a decision. They may be able to help sort out the difficulties in your relationship and can be a source of emotional and practical support if you and your partner decide to split up. Another source of help is friends – particularly those who have been through the process of splitting up themselves.

While only you and your partner can decide whether to continue living together or to split up, others will be affected by the decision and you should bear their interests in mind. Any children will obviously be very much affected, but staying together for the sake of the children is not necessarily the right answer. It may be better for them to be upset for a short period, but grow up in a home free of tension. Your and your partner's parents will also be concerned about keeping in touch with their grandchildren.

Organisations which can help

There are many organisations offering information, advice and counselling services for people considering splitting up.

- Citizens Advice Bureaux

- Marriage counsellors

- Family Mediation Scotland

- CALM

- Women's Aid

- Shelter

- One Parent Families Scotland

- Local authority housing department

- Housing association

- Benefits Agency

- Child Support Agency

- Gingerbread

Citizens Advice Bureaux

A Citizens Advice Bureau offers free, confidential advice, help and information. It is probably the best general source of help. Many bureaux offer free legal advice sessions as well. There are 59 Citizens Advice Bureaux in Scotland. Their telephone numbers and addresses are in local phone books. Information about your nearest bureau can be obtained from:

Citizens Advice Scotland
26 George Square
Edinburgh EH8 9LD
Tel.: 0131-667 0156
Fax: 0131-668 4359

Marriage counsellors

Marriage counsellors provide a confidential service for people who are having difficulty in their marriage or other personal relationships. You can obtain help even if you are definitely thinking of splitting up and you will not be advised to seek a reconciliation or make your relationship work whatever the cost. There are Marriage Guidance Counselling Services throughout Scotland with centres where trained marriage counsellors can be seen. Interviews are usually by appointment. You can find out the address of your local branch from your phone book or local Citizens Advice Bureau or:

> Marriage Counselling Scotland
> 105 Hanover Street
> Edinburgh EH2 1OJ
> Tel.: 0131–225 5006
> Fax: 0131–220 0639

There are also a number of Marriage Guidance Advisory centres for Catholics in different parts of Scotland which offer help on all aspects of family life. Further information can be obtained from:

> Scottish Marriage Care
> 196 Clyde Street
> Glasgow G1 4JY
> Tel.: 0141–204 1239

Family Mediation Scotland

This organisation offers assistance to couples and their families who are splitting up, whether or not they are married. The mediator interviews you and your partner, usually together but sometimes separately, to enable you both to reach an agreement on all matters concerning the breakdown of your relationship, particularly those involving the children. You can either contact the service directly yourself or ask your solicitor to refer you. There may be fees payable for the service, depending on your income. The headquarters office will tell you if there is a service in your area. Most regions in Scotland are covered. More information from:

> Family Mediation Scotland
> 127 Rose St South Lane
> Edinburgh EH2 4BB
> Tel.: 0131–220 1610
> Fax: 0131–220 6895

CALM

CALM is a group of Comprehensive Accredited Lawyer Mediators. The mediators in the group offer comprehensive mediation on all aspects of the breakdown of your relationship. Although all members of the group are qualified solicitors who specialise in family law they could not act for you after providing the mediation if you wanted to proceed with a legal separation or a divorce. However, they could refer you to another solicitor.

You may find it simpler to legally end your relationship if many of the problems about money, property and children have been resolved at mediation. Fees for mediation are the normal hourly rate for a solicitor as set by the Law Society. However, from 1997 for a period of three years, if you qualify for legal aid you could qualify to have the fees of a lawyer mediator paid too. There are members of CALM throughout Scotland. To check if there is someone in your area contact:

The Law Society of Scotland
26 Drumsheugh Gardens
Edinburgh EH3 7YR
Tel.: 0131-226-7411
Fax: 0131-225 2934

Women's Aid

Women's Aid run refuges or safe houses for abused women and their children which provide a safe place for you to stay in while you decide what to do next. Women's Aid also provide useful information including advice on your legal rights, housing options and emotional support. They operate on a 24 hour basis. To contact your nearest Women's Aid Group look in your phone book or contact your local Citizens Advice Bureau or:

Scottish Women's Aid
Norton Park
57 Albion Road
Edinburgh EH7 SQY
Tel.: 0131-475 2372
Fax: 0130-475 2384
Helpline: 0131-475 2372

Shelter

Shelter offers help and information about housing through their housing aid centres. To find your local centre look in your phone book or contact:

> Shelter
> 4th Floor
> Scotiabank House
> 6 South Charlotte Street
> Edinburgh EH2 4AW
> Tel.: 0131-473 7170
> Fax: 0131-473 7199

One Parent Families Scotland

It gives advice and information to single parents or those helping them. It also keeps information on independent self-help groups for single parents throughout Scotland. It can be contacted at:

> One Parent Families Scotland
> 13 Gayfield Square
> Edinburgh EH1 3NX
> Tel.: 0131-556 3899
> Fax: 0131-557 9650

Housing departments

Your local authority housing department can give you advice on getting a house, housing benefit, and, if you and/or your partner are already in one of their houses, having the tenancy transferred to you. If you and your partner can agree that one of you should have the house as a sole tenancy you will have to sort out what to do about any rent arrears

Housing associations

If there is a housing association in the area it may be possible to rent a property from it. Many associations provide housing for people wth special needs.

Benefits Agency

The Benefits Agency runs a confidential service giving advice on benefits. Contact your local office by looking up Benefits Agency or Social Security in the telephone directory.

Child Support Agency

The Child Support Agency operates an enquiry line which is charged at local rates and is open Monday to Friday, 9am to 5pm. The number is 0345 133133.

Gingerbread

This is a self-help organisation for one-parent families, which also offers counselling services and a legal clinic. Your local Citizens Advice Bureau will be able to tell you if there is a group in your area, or contact:

> Scottish Gingerbread Office
> Community Centre Halls
> 304 Maryhill Road
> Glasgow G20 7YE
> Tel.: 0141-353 0989
> Fax: 0141-332 7198

Other sources of help

People or organisations you could turn to for help include your church, doctor, health visitor, the Samaritans, and your local authority social workers. Support for people with problems is thinnest on the ground in rural areas, but you may find that your local Council of Voluntary Service can assist you. Appendix 4 contains a list of publications which you might find helpful.

Solicitors

Do I need a solicitor?

You will generally need the services of a solicitor if you decide to split up. You may need to get a court order or formal agreement for maintenance for yourself or you and your partner may need to sell your home and buy other accommodation. Or you may need to go to court, if you cannot agree, about where the children are going to live and who will be having contact with them. Finally, you will generally need to use a solicitor if you want to start divorce proceedings.

You should think about consulting a solicitor before deciding whether to split up. He or she can advise you about your legal rights on a number of issues (such as occupancy of the family home or where the children should live). This information will put you in a better position to talk things over and reach an agreement with your partner. See Appendix 2 for how to find a solicitor.

A solicitor can offer a fixed fee initial interview. This can be used to identify and explore your problems

Legal aid

If you cannot afford to pay for a solicitor yourself you can be helped through two different schemes:

- Legal advice and assistance - for advice and pre-court work;

- Legal aid - for court work.

A list of solicitors in your area who take part in these schemes can be obtained from the Law Society of Scotland, 26 Drumsheugh Gardens, Edinburgh EH3 7YR (tel.: 0131-226 7411) or your local Citizens Advice Bureau or Sheriff Court.

Further details of these two legal aid schemes are given in Appendix 1.

CHAPTER TWO

EMERGENCY SITUATIONS

This chapter tells you how to deal with situations where you must act quickly in order to get the help you need.

Dealing with violent or threatening behaviour

Informal methods
Involving the police
Telling your partner to leave
Getting an interdict from the court
Getting an exclusion order from the court
Action under the Protection from Harassment Act 1997

What to do if your partner puts you out

Emergency accommodation

Protecting the children

Children being taken elsewhere in the UK
Children being taken out of the UK

Getting money

Protecting your money

Your partner tries to sell the home or give up the tenancy

Your partner is the sole owner or tenant
You and your partner are joint owners or tenants
Your partner stops paying for the home
Safeguarding your belongings
Preventing your partner from removing basic furniture

Dealing with violent or threatening behaviour

Your partner may assault you, threaten you or otherwise make your life so unpleasant that you have to leave home. Since the victim of violent or threatening behaviour is normally a woman, the sections dealing with these topics are written on this basis. But the advice applies equally to a man subjected to such treatment. You can:

- try to stop it informally; *or*

- call the police; *or*

- if you are the sole owner or tenant and you and your partner are not married to each other, tell him to leave; *or*

- obtain an interdict prohibiting your partner from behaving in that way; *or*

- get a court order excluding your partner from the home.

Informal methods

If the violent or threatening behaviour has only just begun you may be able to get your partner to stop it without having to take legal proceedings. You could talk it over with him and say that unless the violence or threats stop you will call the police or go to court. You may find it helpful to involve a friend or relative or a counselling service or Women's Aid if you do not feel like tackling your partner directly.

Another approach is to get your solicitor to write a warning letter to your partner. This may prove effective as it will make it clear that you are seriously considering further action unless things improve.

It is unlikely that talking things over will help if your partner has been maltreating you for some time. In these cases you will need to take legal proceedings to protect yourself. It may be advisable to stay away from home (in a Women's Aid or other refuge for example) to avoid further violence while the court action is in progress.

Involving the police

Physical assaults and threats of violence are criminal offences even when they take place in the home. The fact that the offender and victim are married or cohabiting makes no difference. An offence may be committed even if there is no actual or threatened violence. For instance creating a noisy scene can amount to a breach of the peace. It can also be an offence for your partner to harass you in order to get you to leave if you are entitled to live in the home.

You can call the police if you are assaulted, threatened or there is a scene. The main advantage of the police is that they are available at any time of the day or night. However, for a variety of reasons they may be reluctant to become involved in what they see as domestic disputes. The police will not normally arrest your partner unless your version of the incident is corroborated in some way. Corroboration does not mean that there has to be another eyewitness to the incident. Your injuries, signs of a struggle about the home or screams and shouts heard by neighbours could be sufficient.

If the police arrest your partner this may only be a short-term solution. He will usually be kept in custody overnight and be released the next morning after a brief appearance in court. His trial will be held later and you will be required to give evidence if he pleads not guilty. If your partner is found guilty he will normally be fined. Imprisonment is usually only imposed for serious or repeated assaults. Being arrested, tried and sentenced will not necessarily stop your partner from repeating his violent behaviour when he returns home. On the other hand an appearance in court may deter an otherwise law-abiding man, and a conviction will be useful if you decide to apply for an exclusion order later.

There are some schemes whereby violent people have to go to therapy and group sessions. It seems to work as well as imprisonment.

When no arrest is made the police will attempt to calm things down. They may warn your partner that if the conduct occurs again he will be arrested.

You can complain, either personally or through a solicitor, to the Chief Constable or the Procurator Fiscal if you think the police did not take the appropriate action in response to your call. However this is unlikely to produce a favourable result. You could also let your local Women's Aid group or similar organisation know of your experience; they may be prepared to approach the police if they receive similar complaints from several people.

Telling your partner to leave

If you are the sole owner or tenant and you and your partner are not married to each other, you can simply tell him to leave. Unless your partner has previously been granted occupancy rights (see p31–32) by the court he has no right to remain in the home once you have told him to leave. It is not clear whether you are legally obliged to give your partner a reasonable time to move out. However, you are unlikely to face legal proceedings if you allow your partner a few days (or less if he has been violent) to remove his belongings and find alternative accommodation. If your partner refuses to leave, you can either change the locks on the door or apply to the court for an order requiring him to leave. Once this order has been granted, sheriff officers can be instructed to remove your partner and his belongings from the home, by force if necessary. It may be a good idea to move out until your partner has gone.

You can only take this course of action where your partner has no occupancy rights. If he has occupancy rights because he is a (joint) owner or tenant, or is married to you, or has been granted occupancy rights by a court order, you will have to go to court for an exclusion order (see p17) or recall of the occupancy rights granted to get him out.

Getting an interdict from the court

An interdict is a court order prohibiting the person named in it from doing certain acts specified in the order or being in a specified area, such as the home or stair. You can obtain an interdict prohibiting your partner from assaulting, threatening or molesting you. You can apply for an interdict whether you and your partner are married or cohabiting or living together or apart.

If you are married you can get a special kind of interdict against your husband called a matrimonial interdict. The main advantage of this is that a power of arrest can be attached to it (see below).

If you are not married you can still get an interdict, but you can only get a matrimonial interdict if you and your partner are joint owners or tenants or the court has granted one of you occupancy rights.

A solicitor's help is needed to obtain an interdict from the court, usually the local sheriff court. The court will usually grant you an interdict against violence or molestation fairly readily, especially if you can show you have been ill-treated before.

As soon as your application has been lodged in court you can ask the court to grant an *Interim Interdict*. This will give you immediate protection and will last until your interdict application is heard (generally in a week or so). An interim interdict is usually granted without notice of your application being given to your partner. If you want a power of arrest to be attached to it, your partner has to be given an opportunity to put his case to the court first.

If your partner knowingly does what the interdict prohibits he is said to have breached the interdict. With the help of your solicitor you can report the breach to the court. Breach of interdict is punishable by a fine or imprisonment, but a first offender is usually called to court and given a warning.

Where your interdict has a *Power of Arrest* attached to it the police can arrest your partner without a warrant if they suspect him of having breached the interdict, by assaulting you or loitering on the stair for example. A power of arrest may make the police readier to take positive action in response to your call. However, the police only have a power to arrest; they do not have to use this power in every case and may not do so in yours. You can complain, either personally or through your solicitor, to the Chief Constable or the Procurator Fiscal if you think the police should have arrested your partner.

If your partner is arrested for breach of a matrimonial interdict he will be taken to the police station. The police will then either release him or if further violence seems likely, keep him in custody until he is brought before the court, usually the next morning. If your partner is kept in custody but the Procurator Fiscal decides not to take criminal proceedings, the fiscal applies to the sheriff for your partner to be kept in custody for a further two days. The sheriff will grant this application if satisfied that there was a breach of interdict about which you are going to take legal proceedings and that there is a substantial risk of further violence. In practice, very few applications are granted as sheriffs are not told that legal proceedings for breach of interdict will be brought by the victims.

Even if the police do not arrest your partner or they arrest and then release him, you can still bring legal proceedings for breach of interdict.

Getting an exclusion order from the court

An exclusion order is a court order which suspends your partner's right to occupy the home. It is granted along with orders to remove him from the home, by force if necessary, and to prevent him returning without your permission. You will need the help of a solicitor to apply for an exclusion order.

It will usually take a few months before your application for an exclusion order is heard, as it is almost certain to be opposed by your partner. In the meantime you can apply for an *Interim Exclusion Order* to exclude your partner until the case is heard. An interim exclusion order will not be granted unless your partner has been given an opportunity to challenge it. Before it grants an interim exclusion order or an exclusion order the court must be satisfied that the order is necessary to protect you or your children from any conduct (or threatened or reasonably apprehended conduct) by your partner which injures or could injure your physical or mental health or that of your children. Even where you can show that there is a danger of physical or mental cruelty the court still looks at all the circumstances of the case to make sure that your partner's exclusion would be reasonable. For further information see p35–36.

You can ask the local authority to apply for an exclusion order. It will only do so if it is sure that children are at risk. When the local authority applies for an exclusion order the court will have to be satisfied that the order is necessary and will consider the circumstances primarily in relation to the children.

Action under the Protection from Harassment Act 1997

If your partner or ex-partner harasses you, you can apply to the court for an interdict or a non–harassment order against future harassment. Damages can also be awarded for past harassment. Harassment is conduct that is intentional which occurred on at least two occasions and which a reasonable person would consider amounts to harassment. It includes stalking, persistent telephone calls and loitering outside your home or office. A breach of a non–harassment order is a criminal offence and has to be reported to the police for further action. Non-harassment orders (unlike powers of arrest attached to matrimonial interdicts) do not lapse on divorce and can be obtained against ex–spouses.

What to do if your partner puts you out

If your partner throws you out or changes the locks on the door so you cannot get in, you could try to talk to him directly, or through a friend or relative, to see if you can return at least on a temporary basis. It may be a good idea to wait a few hours to allow tempers to cool.

Alternatively, you can

Break in: This is not advisable unless you are an owner or tenant and you can do it without causing a breach of the peace.

Call the police: Although the police can arrest your partner they are more likely to persuade him to let you back into the house by pointing out that putting you out is a criminal offence. The police may be more willing to take action if you are a (joint) owner or tenant than if you merely have occupancy rights.

There is only one situation where your partner does not commit an offence by putting you out. This is where:

- you and your partner are not married to each other; *and*

- you are not a (joint) owner or tenant or the court has not granted you occupancy rights; *and*

- you have been asked to move out and refused to do so.

Even in this case the police may try to persuade your partner to let you back in temporarily if you have nowhere else to go, and they may help you collect your belongings. If you want to live in the house you will have to apply to the court for occupancy rights (see p31–33).

Apply to the court for an order reinstating you: If you are a (joint) owner or tenant the court will order your partner to let you back into the home, unless your partner can satisfy the court that your behaviour was so bad (violence or heavy drinking for example) that you should be kept out. If you have only occupancy rights (that is you are not a (joint) owner or tenant) the court looks at all circumstances of the case before deciding whether or not it is reasonable that you should be allowed to return.

If you have nowhere else to live, or if the children need you to look after them, your application is likely to be granted. You should apply to the court at once as delay will weaken your case. You can also ask the court, in the event of its ordering your partner to allow you back in, to interdict (prohibit) your partner from putting you out, or threatening to put you out again.

If you and your partner are not married to each other and you are not a (joint) owner or tenant, you will have to apply to the court for occupancy rights (see p31–33). Once the court has granted these you can apply for an order reinstating you, and your partner can be interdicted from shutting you out again. You should not delay in applying for occupancy rights as the court will only grant your application if you are living in the home, or have recently been living there. An application for occupancy rights takes about 12 weeks to be heard. It is not clear whether you can be granted interim rights while your application is being processed.

Claim compensation: You can apply to the court for an order requiring your partner to pay you money as compensation for the cost of finding alternative accommodation and for the loss of your right to occupy the home. In practice this remedy is not much use because most people who throw their partners out are not worth suing. You cannot claim compensation if you are not a (joint) owner or tenant, or you did not have occupancy rights before you were put out.

Emergency accommodation

The sort of accommodation available to you may depend on whether you are on your own or have the children with you and how long you are likely to be there for.

The choices are:–

Friends or relations

Local authority or housing association accommodation: Sometimes these bodies have houses which are available for letting to people on a short term basis. Ask your local authority housing department or a housing association in your area. If you are homeless and are a priority case your local authority has an obligation to provide you (and your children) with temporary accommodation while they are making enquiries into your case (see p37 for further details and provision of permanent accommodation).

Women's aid refuges: These are houses run by Women's Aid but are not available in every part of Scotland. (See p9 for how to contact Women's Aid).

Private rented property: Furnished flats or houses are available through estate or accommodation agencies or advertisements in newspapers or local newsagents. This sort of accommodation can be expensive but you can claim Housing Benefit (see p82) to help pay the rent. Social Fund crisis loans and budgeting loans (see p81) may be available from the Benefits Agency to pay rent in advance, but not returnable deposits.

Hotels or bed and breakfast: This type of accommodation is not suitable for children and benefits may not pay the full cost.

A community care grant (see p80) may be available from the Benefits Agency for moving expenses and necessary household items.

Protecting the children

If you think your partner is likely to remove the children from your care in order to take them to live with him or her, or less commonly to take them abroad, you can apply to the court for:

- an interdict prohibiting removal of the children from your care and control; *or*

- an interdict prohibiting removal of the children from Scotland. You can apply for this interdict even though the children are living in Scotland with your partner.

If the children are living with you it would give the children greater protection from abduction if you had a residence order. This is likely to take about 12 weeks to be considered by the court but an interdict can be available quickly. If your partner continues to threaten to abduct the children you might want to ask the court to take away his or her parental responsibilities and rights.

Do not delay in applying for an interdict if the children are about to be taken abroad. In urgent cases an interdict can be obtained at any hour of the day or night.

Children being taken elsewhere in the UK

Your husband or wife does not commit a criminal offence by taking the children away from you unless force was used or the children are to be taken abroad (see p22). An unmarried father may commit an offence unless he has been awarded parental responsibilities and rights for the children. If no criminal offence has been committed the police will not intervene and you should see your solicitor.

Contact your solicitor promptly if your partner takes the children away from you in breach of an interdict prohibiting this or if you have sole parental responsibilities and rights. Your solicitor will arrange for the matter to be reported to the court. The court will order your partner to return the children and, if an interdict was breached, punish him or her for contempt. This takes the form of a fine or imprisonment, although a first offender is normally called to court and given a warning. If your partner fails to return the children, sheriff officers can be called in to search for them and hand them back to you.

If the children have been taken to another part of the UK, your solicitor will arrange for the appropriate action to be taken there to recover them.

If you did not have an interdict and each of you share parental responsibilities and rights you will have to apply to the court in order to get the children back.

Children being taken out of the UK

Your partner commits a criminal offence by taking or attempting to take the children out of the UK without your consent if you have a residence order in relation to the children or an interdict prohibiting their removal from Scotland or any other part of the United Kingdom. Your partner is liable to be fined or imprisoned and can be extradited from many countries to stand trial in Scotland. Sheriff officers and the police can be asked to assist in tracing the children and preventing their removal from the country.

You can also request the Passport Office in Glasgow not to issue a passport for the children without your consent, but the children may already have passports or be on your partner's passport. The police can be asked to place the children on a "stop list" and alert the immigration authorities at all airports and seaports. If the children are detected their emigration will be prevented. The "stop list" should only be used if there is a real risk of removal; you should not use it merely as a precautionary measure.

Once the children are out of the UK it can be hard to recover them. It may be difficult to trace them, you may have to contest your rights in the other country's courts and legal aid may not be available. However some 50 countries including most European countries and Australia, Canada and the USA have signed international conventions on child abduction and custody. More countries are signing every year. If your children have been taken to one of these countries the authorities in Scotland will contact the authorities there who will endeavour to trace them and if successful will arrange for your parental responsibilities and rights to be recognised and enforced. Your solicitor will advise you on what action to take.

Further advice

Reunite: Reunite is an organisation which provides practical help and support to parents who have had a child abducted overseas or who fear abduction may occur. It can also put you in touch with other parents who have been in the same situation. The address is :-

Reunite
National Council for Abducted Children
PO Box 4
London WC1X 3DX
Tel.: 0171-404 8356
Fax: 0171-242 1512

Getting money

If you and/or the children are left without any money you may be able to get money from:

The Benefits Agency: You can claim Income Support (or Jobseekers Allowance from the Employment Service if you have to be available for work) for yourself and any children if you are not working (see p76 for further details). If you are in need of money immediately you may be able to get a Social Fund crisis loan from the Benefits Agency to tide you over until your benefit is paid (see p80). If you are working you may be able to claim Family Credit (see p81).

Your local authority social work office: They may be able to help if the Benefits Agency cannot.

Child support or maintenance

Your partner: You can apply for financial support for your children through the Child Support Agency from their other parent. In addition you can apply to the court for an order requiring your husband or wife to pay aliment, the Scottish legal term for maintenance, for you. Once your application is lodged you can ask the court to award a weekly or monthly amount called *Interim aliment.* This interim aliment lasts until your application for aliment is heard. You can use this method if you know your partner's whereabouts and he or she has the means to pay.

Loans: Your bank may allow you to overdraw your account but you will have to satisfy them that you will be able to pay it back eventually. Your friends and family may be prepared to lend you money, but again you should think about how you are going to repay them. Do not borrow from money lenders if you can possible avoid it. Their rates of interest are very high and the other terms of the loan may be unfavourable.

Selling or pawning your belongings: The drawback is that it will cost you a lot more to replace them later on. It is a criminal offence to sell your partner's belongings or items which you both own without permission. See p42 for what is likely to be jointly owned.

Protecting your money

If you have a joint account with your partner there is a danger that your partner will withdraw all the money from it. You can prevent this by:

- withdrawing all or part of the money yourself, *or*

- contacting the bank or building society. Some organisations will then not allow withdrawals to be made unless both you and your partner sign the withdrawal form or cheques.

- stop credit cards. If one partner has the main card and the other has a subsidiary card, the main card holder can cancel the subsidiary card.

Your partner tries to sell the home or give up the tenancy

Your partner may try to sell the home or give up the tenancy. The way in which you are protected against this depends on whether you are a (joint) owner or tenant and whether you and your partner are married to each other.

Your partner is the sole owner or tenant

Married: You must consent in writing to any sale or giving up of the tenancy unless you have renounced your occupancy rights (see p31). As long as you have not consented or renounced you are entitled to continue living there. Your consent may be dispensed with if the court, on an application by your husband or wife, is satisfied that you are withholding consent unreasonably. You would be acting unreasonably for example if you did not want to continue living in the home and refused consent out of spite.

Cohabiting: Your partner can give up the tenancy or sell the house without your consent. If you think this is likely you should apply to the court for an order giving you occupancy rights (see p31), if you have not already got such an order. Once you have got occupancy rights you can ask the court to grant an interdict prohibiting your partner from selling or giving up the tenancy. Unless you act quickly the tenancy may have been given up or the home sold, and you will not be able to reverse matters.

Some local authorities do not require a sole tenant's husband or wife to consent to the tenant giving up the tenancy. If you find your husband or wife has given up the tenancy and you want to stay on in or return to the home, you should contact the housing department at once. Point out that you are legally entitled to continue living in the property.

You and your partner are joint owners or tenants

Married: You must consent in writing to any sale or giving up of the tenancy. See p24 for the court's power to dispense with your consent. In the case of an owner-occupied home your husband or wife could alternatively apply to the court for an order requiring it to be sold. The court may however refuse to order a sale or postpone it until the children no longer need it, for example.

Cohabiting: Your partner can give up the tenancy for both without your consent. If this seems likely you should apply to the court for an interdict prohibiting your partner from doing this. Act quickly otherwise you will be too late. The home cannot be sold unless you and your partner join in the sale. The exception is where the court grants an order for sale. The court has no power to refuse or postpone this order if your partner applies for it.

Your partner stops paying for the home

Tenants: If your partner stops paying the rent, the landlord will almost certainly take steps to bring the tenancy to an end. Once this has been done you have no further rights to remain in the home. In order to continue to live in the home you will therefore have to pay the rent legally due by your partner. You do not need your partner's permission to pay the rent, and the landlord is bound to accept rent offered by you.

As soon as you realise the rent is not being paid you should get in touch with the landlord and offer to pay the rent. See if they will agree to some arrangement for paying off the arrears by instalments. If legal proceedings for non-payment of rent have already been started, you are entitled to go along to the court in order to object as if you were the tenant. The court will not usually order eviction if you offer to pay off the arrears by reasonable instalments. You do not need your partner's permission to take these steps.

Where you and your partner are joint tenants each of you may be called on to pay the whole rent. Failure to pay the whole amount will mean that the landlord can take steps to bring the tenancy to an end and evict you.

You may be able to get help with the rent by way of Housing Benefit (see p82). Another solution is to apply to the court for an order requiring your partner to reimburse you for the rent and arrears you paid on his or her behalf. You will probably not get the full amount back as you are getting the benefit of living in the home.

To prevent further trouble over non-payment of rent you could consider becoming the tenant in place of your partner or having the joint tenancy transferred to your name alone (see p32).

Owners: If your partner stops paying the monthly repayments due to the building society, bank or other lender they will eventually call up the loan. This means the whole loan (not just the arrears) has to be repaid, otherwise they will evict you and sell the home. Your partner would be ill-advised to stop paying the instalments, since non-payers are blacklisted and may find it difficult to get credit in future. Also the home is unlikely to fetch as much in a forced sale as it would if sold normally.

Once you realise or suspect that payments are not being made you should contact the building society, bank or other lender as soon as possible if you want to continue living in the home, and explain the position to them. You are entitled to make the payments yourself and you do not need your partner's permission to do this. The lender may also require you to agree to pay off any arrears by instalments if they decide not to call up the loan.

Where you and your partner are joint borrowers each of you may be called on to pay the whole of the monthly instalments. Failure to pay the whole amount will result in the calling up of the loan and the sale of the home.

Some help with the monthly payments may be obtained from Income Support (see p76), Another solution is to apply to the court for an order requiring your partner to reimburse you for the money you have paid the lender on his or her behalf. You will probably not get the full amount back from your partner as you are getting the benefit of living in the home. If you cannot afford to keep up the payments see a solicitor and sell the home yourself. Try to avoid it being sold by the lender as they will usually not get such a good price.

Safeguarding your belongings

If your partner threatens to dispose of your belongings or refuses to hand them over to you, you can apply to the court. The court can grant an interdict prohibiting your partner from disposing of your belongings, or order your partner to hand over your belongings to you. If you are frightened to go in you could ask a friend to get them for you, or instruct a sheriff officer to collect them. In urgent cases an interdict will be granted as soon as you apply. What are your belongings and what are your partner's is often difficult to decide (see p42 for further details).

If you are a (joint) owner or tenant you can use the home to store your belongings in, as long as this does not interfere with your partner's enjoyment of the property as a residence.

If you are not a (joint) tenant or owner, but have occupancy rights, you can bring reasonably required household goods into the home and your partner cannot insist that you remove them if you leave temporarily. You cannot use your partner's home as a storeroom for non-household goods, or for items you acquire after you leave, without your partner's permission.

Preventing your partner from removing basic furniture

If you have a right to occupy the home (as a sole or joint owner or tenant or a person with occupancy rights) you can secure your use of furniture and contents which belong to your partner. After all, it is not much use being entitled to live in the home if your partner can take everything away. You have to apply to the court for an order allowing you use and possession of various items. It may also be useful to apply for an interdict prohibiting your partner from removing any of these items without your agreement. The various items must be such as are reasonably necessary to enable you to use the home as a residence. For example, your partner would be able to remove books and a piano but not beds, tables or chairs.

CHAPTER THREE

SORTING OUT
ACCOMMODATION

This chapter deals with your and your partner's legal rights concerning the home and suggests sources of alternative accommodation.

Staying put

Am I entitled to stay in the home?
Finding out if you are a (joint) tenant or owner
Married to the tenant or owner
Living with the tenant or owner
Can the tenancy be transferred to me?
Am I liable to pay council tax?
Can I do repairs or improvements?
Can I get my partner out?
Exclusion orders

Moving out

Where can I find somewhere to live?
Your rights if you are homeless
Your new home and your former partner

When you and your partner have decided to end your relationship and split up, one of the most important questions is where each of you is going to live. The choices are:

- you leave while your partner remains in the home; *or*

- your partner leaves while you remain in the home; *or*

- both of you leave; *or*

- both of you stay in the home.

The last option, both of you staying in the home, is unlikely to be a practical solution unless neither of you can find alternative accommodation or you are planning to move apart in the near future. Once a relationship is at an end it is often difficult for a couple to continue to live separate lives under the same roof.

You should try to agree with your partner who is to remain in the home. Do not rush - you may make a decision which you come to regret later. There is no easy way to decide what to do - each couple has to solve the problem in the light of their own circumstances. In the short term at any rate, it is usually best for the partner who is going to look after the children to remain in the home.

To help you come to a decision, the remainder of this chapter deals with the legal background to your and your partner's rights in the home. Of course legal issues are not the only ones to consider. Moving out is a great upheaval and may mean your losing contact with your friends and familiar surroundings. On the other hand, once you have got over the shock of splitting up, you may look on starting a new life elsewhere as a challenge, or an opportunity to move nearer to your own family. You may also want to move to a completely different part of the country to prevent your partner pestering or molesting you.

Finally, you and your partner cannot normally continue to live at the same standard as you did when you lived together. You should try to ensure that any drop in standards is shared, not borne by you alone.

Staying put

Am I entitled to stay in the home?

You are entitled to continue to occupy and live in the home which you and your partner lived in if:

- you are the owner or tenant or a joint owner or joint tenant; *or*

- you are married to your partner who is the owner or tenant; *or*

- you are not married to your partner who is the owner or tenant, but the court has granted you occupancy rights (see p31); *or*

- you have some other legal right that entitles you to stay there as a tenant of your partner for example.

Your partner may allow you to stay even if you have no legal entitlement, but this permission can be withdrawn at any time. You should be given reasonable notice to leave and your partner has no right to physically throw you and your belongings out on the street without obtaining an ejection order from the court.

If you have a right to live in the home, then you can have any of your children or your partner's children living with you. Your partner is not entitled to exclude the children (including those over 16) with the intention of forcing you to leave.

It is a criminal offence for your partner to harass you in order to get you to leave if you are entitled to stay.

Finding out if you are a (joint) tenant or owner

Many of your rights depend on whether you are a tenant or owner. It is normally easy to find this out.

You are the sole tenant if only your name is on the lease or tenancy agreement, while you and your partner are joint tenants if both your names are there. You or your partner should have a copy of the lease or agreement; if not you should ask the landlord to let you see it. If you are not sure of your position - because for example, there is no written lease or agreement or the original document has been altered verbally later - you should seek advice from a Citizens Advice Bureau or a solicitor.

In the case of owner occupied property, whose name is on the document of title to the property is all important. You will never become the owner simply by paying the bills or making improvements. You are the sole owner if the title is in your name, while if you and your partner are both named you are joint owners. Joint ownership is very common nowadays amongst married and cohabiting couples. Unless the document of title says otherwise each joint owner has an equal share in the property.

If you want to find out about the title to your home you could ask your partner or the solicitor who was involved in the purchase. Another way is to ask at The Registers of Scotland, Meadowbank House, London Road, Edinburgh (tel.: 0131 659 6111) where a copy of the title to any property in Scotland may be inspected on payment of a fee.

In exceptional cases you can be declared to be the owner or joint owner even though you are not mentioned in the title. These are if:

- the person mentioned in the title accepts, or the court is satisfied that there was an agreement that you were to be entitled to the home or a share of it; *or*

- you prove that your name has been omitted from the title by mistake or fraud.

These are very uncommon situations.

Married to the tenant or owner

Where your husband or wife is the sole owner or tenant of the home you are entitled to continue to live in it or to return to live in it. However, if your husband or wife won't let you in you will have to apply to the court for an order enforcing your rights (see p19). These rights called occupancy rights normally last as long as you remain married, unless you renounce them (see below) or they have been suspended by a court order (see exclusion order on p17). When you and your husband or wife get divorced the court dealing with the divorce can continue your occupancy rights.

Where your husband or wife is only a joint owner or tenant but you are not the other joint owner or tenant, you have occupancy rights in the home only if the other joint owner or tenant is not living in the house as well. For example, if you and your wife live in a house owned jointly by your wife and her mother, you will have occupancy rights only as long as your mother-in-law is not living with you.

You can lose your occupancy rights by agreeing to renounce them – give them up. To be effective a renunciation must be in writing and signed in front of a notary public (most solicitors are notaries) and witnesses. Before you sign the notary must be satisfied that you are giving up your rights freely and not as the result of undue pressure. There are very few circumstances in which it will be in your interest to give up your rights. You are strongly advised never to renounce your rights without first seeking independent advice. While you are happily married occupancy rights may seem unimportant, but they can be extremely valuable on splitting up.

Living with the tenant or owner

If your partner is the sole owner or tenant and you are not married to him or her, you have no right to continue to live in the home once you have been asked to leave but you can apply to the court for an order granting you occupancy rights. You will need a solicitor to apply for the order on your behalf. If you have left the home you should apply promptly. A long delay may mean that the court will not grant your application.

The court first decides whether you and your partner are cohabiting – living together as if you were husband and wife. You are likely to be regarded as cohabiting if you have lived together for more than a year and/or you and your partner have had children. The court goes on to consider whether you should be given the right to live in your partner's home. Important factors are your, your partner's and any children's need for accommodation and the possibility of your obtaining some other suitable place to live. If you are looking after young children you will very probably be allowed to stay on in the home.

It takes about 12 weeks for your application for occupancy rights to be dealt with by the court. It is not clear whether interim occupancy rights are available so if your partner will not let you live in the home, you may have to find somewhere else to live for this period.

The occupancy rights the court grants you last for 6 months initially. You can however apply for further extensions, which last for 6 months at a time. The court is most unlikely to allow you to stay on indefinitely by repeatedly renewing your occupancy rights, especially if your partner owns the home.

Can the tenancy be transferred to me?

On splitting up you may want the tenancy of the home to be in your name, instead of your partner's or jointly with your partner. This can be done by applying to the landlord or the court.

As long as your partner and the landlord agree, the tenancy can be made over to you. Although you are not legally responsible for any arrears of rent due by your partner, in practice the landlord may try to "persuade" you to pay them. See a solicitor if this happens.

Where the home is rented from a public sector landlord (local authority) , Scottish Homes, housing association etc) and your partner refuses to transfer you can ask the landlord to apply to the court for an order terminating your partner's tenancy or joint tenancy. Partner includes ex-husband or ex-wife. The court will grant this order if satisfied that other suitable accommodation is available for your partner and that the home is to be re-let to you because you and your partner don't want to live together. Unless you are divorced you can also use the procedure described below. You have to use that procedure if the landlord is not a public sector landlord or won't agree to apply.

Where your partner and/or the landlord refuse to agree to the transfer you can apply to the court for a tenancy transfer order, either separately or as part of your separation or divorce proceedings. To apply you have to be married to the tenant or be a cohabiting partner with occupancy rights (see p31)but you can apply for occupancy rights at the same time as you apply for a tenancy transfer order. In deciding whether or not to grant a tenancy transfer order, the court looks at all the circumstances. Attention is paid to both your and your partner's needs for accommodation and ability to find other accommodation. Where there are children their needs are usually the deciding factor. If you need the home for yourself and the children the court will almost certainly give you the tenancy. The landlord is entitled to object to your application. While the court will listen to arguments about your inability to pay the rent or be a good tenant, it may overrule them. You should be prepared to satisfy the court that the landlord's fears are groundless or exaggerated. You can get help with the rent through Housing Benefit (see p82).

Once you become the tenant in place of your partner you are then liable to pay the rent and carry out the other conditions of the lease – keeping the garden tidy, or not annoying the neighbours for example. But you are not liable for any arrears of rent due by your partner. As the new tenant you can require your ex-husband/wife or cohabiting partner to leave the home, but to get your husband or wife out legally an exclusion order (see p17) is necessary.

Your partner's share of a joint tenancy with you can be transferred so that you become the sole tenant. This can be done by agreement or by application to the court as above.

Am I liable to pay council tax?

Persons over 18 solely or mainly resident in a local authority area have to pay council tax to the local authority for the property in which they live. The amount is normally payable in monthly instalments.

A married or cohabiting couple are jointly and severally liable for council tax while they are living together. This means that if your partner fails to pay his share of the council tax, you can be made to pay the whole amount.

When your partner moves out, you become responsible for paying council tax on the property. Council tax bills are based on the assumption that two adults live in the property. If you are the only adult, or other adults fall into certain categories, for example, students or YT trainees, you should apply for a 25% single person's discount on your council tax. You may also be eligible for council tax benefit (see p82) depending on your income. While you are living with your partner any rebate is based on your joint income. Once you have separated your rebate will be assessed on your income only.

Can I do repairs or improvements?

Your rights depend on whether the home is owned or rented and what sort of right you have to live in it (see below). Bear in mind that improvements involving structural alterations (such as building a garage or knocking two rooms into one) will usually require building control permission and may need planning permission as well. Check with your local authority before you start.

Where the home is rented you may need the landlord's permission to do maintenance, repairs or improvements, or the landlord may be responsible for keeping the property in repair. Check the lease or tenancy agreement and ask the landlord before you start. If the home is rented from the local authority and they are obliged to carry out repairs, you may be able to get modest repairs done yourself and ask them to reimburse you, rather than wait for them to do the work.

You are the sole owner/tenant

You do not need your partner's agreement to do any repairs etc. You can apply to the court for an order requiring your husband or wife (if living in the home) to contribute to the cost of essential repairs (mending a leaking roof or replacing dangerous wiring for example) or repairs he or she has agreed to. If you and your partner are not married you can apply only if he or she has been granted occupancy rights.

You and your partner are joint owners/tenants

You do not need your partner's agreement for essential repairs. If you want to carry out other work and your partner won't agree you can apply to the court for authorisation. Unless the court orders otherwise the cost of any work including essential repairs is shared equally.

You have occupancy rights as the partner of the owner or tenant

You do not need your partner's agreement for essential repairs. You can apply to the court for an order requiring your partner to contribute to the cost. If you want to do non-essential repairs or improvements and your partner won't agree you can apply to the court for authorisation. You will have to pay the whole cost yourself.

You have no occupancy rights

You are not entitled to do any repairs etc without your partner's agreement. If you do you are liable for the whole cost yourself, and you may be required to restore the property to its previous state.

Can I get my partner out?

Being entitled to stay put in the home is only half of the battle, since you will normally want it to yourself. This means your partner has to move out. If it will not provoke violence you could try persuading him or her to go voluntarily before you take any of these steps below. If your partner will not go voluntarily you can:

Shut him or her out:

You will in most cases be committing a criminal offence by doing this and your partner may take legal proceedings against you (sec p19). The exceptional case is where you are the sole owner or tenant AND you and your partner are not married to each other AND your partner has not been granted occupancy rights by the court. Here your partner is obliged to leave once you have told him or her to go. You should however give a reasonable period of notice and you are not entitled to throw your partner and your partner's belongings out into the street without getting an ejection order from the court.

Go to court for an exclusion order:

If you get it your partner will no longer be entitled to live in or be in the home even if he or she is a (joint) owner or tenant.

Exclusion orders

To obtain an exclusion order you will need to demonstrate to the court that it is necessary to protect you or your children from any conduct (or threatened or reasonably apprehended conduct) by your partner that injures or could injure your physical or mental health or that of your children. Even where you satisfy this test, the court still looks at all the circumstances of the case - such as your and your partner's conduct and finances and the needs of any children to make sure that exclusion would be reasonable. A most important factor is the need of the children for suitable accommodation. If you were forced to leave home because of domestic violence and have to live with the children in cramped, temporary accommodation, the court is likely to order your partner out. When the children require protection from abuse the local authority can apply for an exclusion order and if this is granted the abuser can be kept out of the home for 6 months in the first instance. The tests that the court apply in granting an exclusion order when the local authority applies are different. The court will focus largely on the issue of risk of abuse to the children when the local authority is the applicant.

You can apply for an exclusion order while you are still in the home or after you have been forced to leave. Your application for an exclusion order is almost certain to be opposed by your partner, so that your solicitor will need all the supporting evidence that can be obtained. This might include statements from neighbours, police reports of previous incidents, certificates from your doctor as to injuries to your health, and the unsuitable nature of your temporary accommodation if you have moved out. If you can foresee your need for an exclusion order you should try to tell your neighbours and your doctor about your injuries as they occur, and what they were caused by, so that they will be in a position to give evidence later.

Where you and your partner are cohabitees and your partner is the sole owner or tenant you must have occupancy rights (see p31) before the court will consider your application for an exclusion order. However you can apply for occupancy rights and an exclusion order at the same time.

An exclusion order normally lasts until it is cancelled by the court or until divorce (married couples only). However, the divorce court can continue the exclusion order after divorce, but it will only do so if it decides to award you the right after divorce to occupy your ex-husband's or wife's home. If you are a cohabitee and the home is not in your name the court is unlikely to exclude your partner for more than a few months - long enough to enable you to find alternative accommodation or to apply for the tenancy to be transferred to you.

Moving out

Where can I find somewhere to live?

If you decide to leave home you will have to find somewhere else to live. See p20 for emergency accommodation.

The main sources of permanent housing are:

- local authority
- buying your own home
- housing associations
- shared ownership housing
- private landlords
- mobile homes

Local authority: In most areas council houses are in short supply and there will be a waiting list. In particular there is very little accommodation available for single people. Ask your local authority how it gives different people priority for housing. If you count as a person in "priority need " your council may be bound to provide you with permanent accommodation particularly if you have children in need. (see p38).

Housing associations: There are a number of national and local housing associations that provide rented accommodation. It is usually cheaper than other privately rented accommodation. The *Yellow Pages* will give details of associations in your area.

Alternatively contact:

> Scottish Federation of Housing Associations
> 38 York Place
> Edinburgh EH1 3HU
> Tel.: 0131 556 5777

Private rented housing: Accommodation and estate agencies or solicitors are the best sources; newspapers and newsagents also advertise property to let. Private rented accommodation tends to be expensive though Housing Benefit (see p82) is available to help pay the rent. Social Fund Crisis Loans and Budgeting Loans (see p81) may be obtainable from the Benefits

Agency to meet rent in advance. Community Care Grants and Social Fund loans may also be obtainable from the Benefits Agency to meet the cost of basic furniture if you can only find unfurnished accommodation and you have no furniture of your own.

You should also consider what security of tenure you will have. This is a very complex subject. If you are in doubt you should seek advice from a Citizens Advice Bureau or a solicitor.

Owner occupied housing: Buying a house is expensive although it may be better than renting in the long run if you can afford it. You will need some cash even if you can get a loan for most of the price. If you and your partner own your home you may be able to put your share towards a new home for yourself. The amount of loan you can get depends on your income and the value placed on the home you are thinking of buying by the lender's surveyor. You should consult a solicitor before you start looking around, and certainly before you sign any offer to buy, because otherwise you may commit yourself to something you cannot fulfil.

Shared ownership housing: This is a mixture of ownership and tenancy. Shared ownership schemes are not common but may be worth looking for. The amount of loan required is smaller than if you bought the home completely. Contact Scottish Homes, Thistle House, 91 Haymarket Terrace, Edinburgh EH12 5HE (tel.: 0131 313 0044) for further details.

Mobile homes: There are not many sites with caravans that can be occupied all the year round. Most of them tend to be situated away from shops, schools and workplaces. The owner-occupier of a residential caravan is entitled to an agreement with the site owner which gives security of tenure for at least 5 years. A caravan is a depreciating asset so you are unlikely to get back what you paid for it. Housing Benefit is available to help with rent if you rent the caravan or with site rent if you own it.

Your rights if you are homeless

If you are:

- homeless or threatened with homelessness; *and*
- in priority need; *and*
- not intentionally homeless; *and*
- have a local connection; *and*
- not subject to immigration control

your local housing authority is obliged to provide you with (or see that you are provided with) suitable permanent accommodation. The type of permanent accommodation you will be offered varies from authority to authority and the way in which authorities interpret their duties varies also. The local authority also has specific duties to provide accommodation for a homeless young person aged 16 to 21, in certain circumstances. If you are dissatisfied with their decision you can apply to the Court of Session for it to be reviewed.

You are homeless if you have no accommodation or you are unable to use your accommodation because you have been thrown out, or you would run the risk of violence if you lived there. You still count as homeless even if you are staying in a refuge or other emergency accommodation because of the violence at home. On the other hand you will not be regarded as homeless simply because you and your partner have decided to split up and find alternative accommodation.

The term "threatened with homelessness" means that it is likely that you will be homeless within the next 28 days, for example if you are a tenant about to be evicted or have been told by your partner with whom you are cohabiting to leave.

To be in priority need you must:

- have dependent children (which need not be your own, nor is it necessary that the court has awarded you parental rights and responsibilities for them); *or*

- be pregnant; *or*

- have lost your accommodation due to an emergency (such as a fire); *or*

- you or a member of your household are vulnerable as a result of old age, handicap or other special reason.

The Code of Guidance on Homelessness September 1997 by the Scottish Office suggests that women without children who have suffered domestic violence should be regarded as vulnerable. The Code also directs the local authority to accept the expressed fears of someone who is the victim of violence if it is difficult to obtain written evidence of the violence, for example, from a G.P.

If the local authority considers that you are intentionally homeless (you deliberately didn't pay the rent for example) then they need only offer you temporary accommodation. However, the local authority does have a duty to safeguard and promote the welfare of children in its area who are in need. As well as providing services the local authority should at all times be trying to keep families together so if you and the children need accommodation this is what should be provided. The Code of Guidance on Homelessness suggests that victims of domestic violence who have fled their homes should not be treated as intentionally homeless. The local authority may not agree. They may adopt the attitude that victims should stay in the home and apply to the court to have their violent partners excluded or prohibited from treating them violently by interdict or a non-harassment order. If you are faced with this argument you should point out that exclusion orders are difficult to get and that interdicts and non-harassment orders do not necessarily protect you from your partner's violent behaviour.

Normally your application for accommodation would be made to the authority which you have a local connection with (living or working in their area for example). But you can apply for permanent accommodation to another local authority in Scotland, England and Wales in order to escape from your violent partner. As long as you can show that you would be in danger from violence if you stayed in your own area, you need not have a connection with the authority to which you apply.

Your new home and your former partner

When you do find new accommodation for yourself, your former partner has no rights to live in it or to be in it without your consent. This is because it is not a matrimonial home - a home for you and your partner; it is a home you got for yourself (and any children). If your partner attempts to get in, or refuses to leave after you have told him or her to go, you can call the police. You may find the police will deal more sympathetically with your case than if you were still living with your partner, as it is no longer a "domestic dispute".

Another way of dealing with your partner molesting you or causing trouble is to apply to the court for an interdict or a non-harassment order An interdict may be enforced in the same way as other interdicts (see p16) but if you are divorced from your partner or were not married to him or her, you cannot have a power of arrest attached to your interdict. If a non-harassment order is broken, it is a criminal offence and the violent partner could be imprisoned for up to 5 years for breaking it.

CHAPTER FOUR

UNTANGLING YOUR FINANCES AND PROPERTY

This chapter provides guidance for married and cohabiting couples on how to sort out their property and financial affairs.

Who owns the household goods?

Married couples
Cohabiting couples
Disagreements about the belongings
Using your partner's furniture

What about the home?

You and/or your partner rent the home
You and/or your partner own the home

Who owns the savings and investments?

Am I liable for my partner's debts?

Hire purchase goods
Fuel bills
Telephone bill

Who to inform about splitting up

Other tasks to consider

While you and your partner lived together you will have rented or bought a home and bought furnishings and appliances for it. You will also have bought things yourselves and for each other. You may have opened joint accounts with a bank or building society or undertaken joint financial commitments such as a house purchase loan or a hire purchase agreement. On splitting up you will have to work out with your partner what to do about the home, the belongings, savings and financial commitments.

You and your partner should try to agree on these matters if possible. Going to court can be expensive and the legal expenses may easily exceed the value of the items under dispute. Even if you win you may not recover all your expenses from your partner. To help you and your partner to reach a mutually acceptable solution this chapter sets out the legal rules relating to ownership of property and liability for debts.

Who owns the household goods?

Deciding who owns the household goods and similar articles is often very difficult. This is because it may be necessary to think back many years to when the item was bought to find out who bought it and what their intentions were then.

Married couples

Household goods are assumed to belong to the husband and wife equally. Joint ownership is only an assumption; you may still be able to establish that you are the sole owner of a particular item, but the mere fact that you bought it does not help your claim. Household goods means furniture, furnishings and articles such as beds, tables, chairs, carpets, curtains, wardrobes, chests; but also includes pictures, books, refrigerators, televisions, pianos and washing machines. On the other hand money, cars and pets are not counted as household goods.

For joint ownership to be assumed the household goods must have been bought for your and your husband's or wife's "joint domestic purposes" for furnishing the home, for joint use in the home or for child care. If you have golf clubs or a computer for yourself or equipment for your business, these would not have been bought for a joint domestic purpose so that the rule that the person who bought them is normally the owner would apply, (see p43).

Articles which you owned before marriage are not assumed to be joint property. They will continue to belong to you even though they are situated in your husband's or wife's home and both of you use them, unless you have actually given them to your husband or wife or made it clear that they are to be joint property. The assumption of joint ownership also does not apply to items you acquired after you split up.

If someone makes you a gift of an article then it will belong to you. This simple rule can often be difficult to apply because in the case of "gifts" from one spouse to the other the giver may not have made his or her intention clear. Unless your spouse actually made it clear, or it is clear from the nature of the article (such as clothes or jewellery which only you can wear) that a gift was intended, it will be assumed that the article was merely lent to you or that you were simply allowed to use it.

Another difficulty is that where other people give a present it may have been intended for both of you or for only one of you. Who owns it depends on the intention of the giver. Sometimes this is clear from what was said or written at the time of the gift - wedding presents are normally addressed to both bride and groom. Where the giver's intention was not expressed, you have to try and work it out from the nature of the present and the circumstances in which it was given. A birthday present, for instance, is obviously intended for the person whose birthday it is.

Cohabiting couples

As a general rule you are the owner of articles which:

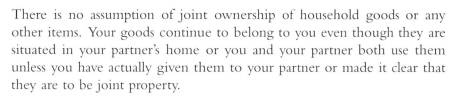

- you acquired before you lived together or after you split up, *or*

- you bought, *or*

- you were given.

There is no assumption of joint ownership of household goods or any other items. Your goods continue to belong to you even though they are situated in your partner's home or you and your partner both use them unless you have actually given them to your partner or made it clear that they are to be joint property.

Normally you own any article which you buy while living with your partner even if you used your partner's money or joint money instead of your own. This rule does not apply if you bought things on behalf of your partner - for example if she asked you to buy a typewriter for her. In this case the article belongs to your partner. Using your partner's money when you have no right to do so could be theft or embezzlement and you could be prosecuted as well as being made to repay the money.

The rules relating to gifts are the same as for married couples (see p43).

Disagreements about the belongings

If you and your partner cannot agree who owns what, or how the belongings are to be divided, you may have to go to court to resolve the dispute. However, the legal expenses may be more than the items are worth, and even if you win you may find yourself out of pocket.

Where your ownership of an article is admitted or proved the court can:

- order your partner to return the article to you or its value if he or she no longer has it; *and*

- authorise sheriff officers to search for the article and hand it over to you; *and*

- interdict (prohibit) your partner from removing or threatening to remove the article from your possession in the future.

If you and your partner are joint owners of an article and you cannot agree what is to happen to it, you can apply to the court for an order requiring the article to be sold and the money divided between you.

The court on granting a divorce has power to order transfers of property. In this way you could become sole owner of items you and your husband or wife own jointly or become the owner of items belonging solely to your husband or wife. Obviously you can only apply to the court if you are married and have grounds for divorce proceedings (see Chapter 8). Another solution is to apply for a use and possession order (see below). This is not tied to divorce proceedings and is available if you are married or cohabiting.

Using your partner's furniture

You can apply to the court for an order (a "use and possession order") allowing you to use in the home your partner's furniture and furnishings which are situated there. You may also wish to apply for an interdict preventing your partner from removing the items you have been given the use of. To qualify you must be entitled to occupy the home either as a (joint) tenant or owner or as a person with occupancy rights. A use and possession order could be very useful if you want to go on living in the home, but all the furniture is your partner's and he or she intends to remove it. An empty house would not be much good to you if you had no means of refurnishing it.

The court can only give you use and possession of items which are reasonably necessary to enable the home to be used as a residence. Things like beds, tables, chairs, cookers, fires, china, cutlery, carpets and curtains sufficient for your (and any children's) needs would be included, but cars are definitely excluded. Whether you would be given the use of items such as a piano, television or a washing machine would depend on your circumstances. For example, if you were looking after very young children a washing machine might be regarded as reasonably necessary.

What about the home?

You and/or your partner rent the home

If neither you nor your partner want to continue to live in the home, it is best to give up the tenancy. This is done by giving notice to the landlord. The period of notice depends on the terms of the lease or tenancy agreement. The landlord may be willing to accept shorter notice; on the other hand, particularly in the case of a fixed term tenancy, the landlord may not be prepared to accept termination before the due date.

If you want to stay on and your partner agrees to this, you could have the tenancy transferred to you (see p32 for how to do this). You should consider carefully whether you can afford to pay the rent and other running costs, since once you become the tenant you will be liable for these. You may be able to get Housing Benefit (see p82) to help with the rent.

Your partner may not agree to your staying on in the home. Your rights to do so and to exclude your partner are dealt with in Chapters 2 and 3. See Chapter 2 also for ways of preventing your partner from bringing the tenancy to an end without your agreement.

You and/or your partner own the home

Selling: If neither you nor your partner want to carry on living in the home after splitting up, it is best to sell it and use the money to get separate accommodation for each of you.

The money from the sale of the home belongs to the owner or to the joint owners (see p30 for how to find out if you are an owner or joint owner). If you are not the owner or a joint owner, and your partner is not prepared to pay part of the proceeds to you when the home is sold you can:

- start divorce proceedings claiming a lump sum or a transfer of the home to you and meanwhile asking the court to make an order prohibiting or preventing a sale or "freezing" the money from a sale.

  This applies if you are married to the sole owner and you have grounds for divorce (see Chapter 8).

- apply to the court for an order requiring your partner to repay to you the money you contributed when the home was bought or improved.

  This applies if you are married to or cohabiting with the sole owner and your contribution was made not more than 5 years from the date of your application. If you are cohabiting you must have occupancy rights or be granted them at the same time (see p31). You may also apply in some other circumstances.

Other methods include:

- refusing to consent to the sale.

  This applies if you have occupancy rights as the husband or wife of the sole owner. Your refusal to consent may however be overruled by the court (see p24).

- applying to the court for occupancy rights and an interdict prohibiting the sale.

  This applies if you are cohabiting with the sole owner.

These methods will not by themselves give you a share of the money. But taking or threatening to take such action may lead to your partner "buying you off". It would be wise to get any agreement about the sharing of money resulting from the sale of the home prepared by a solicitor, so that it can be enforced easily if the need arises.

Staying on: If you want to stay on in the home and your partner is agreeable to this, you may want to become the owner. You should think carefully and seek advice from a solicitor before agreeing to buy the home (or your partner's share in it) from your partner. The building society, bank or other lender will also have to be consulted and agree to the transfer unless their loan is to be paid off. On the other hand you may be content to leave the ownership as it is and simply continue to occupy the home. From your partner's point of view this has the disadvantage of tying up in the home money which he or she may need to buy other accommodation.

Another possibility is for you to forgo your financial claims against your partner in exchange for your partner's (share of the) home. This applies mainly to married couples since cohabiting couples seldom have financial claims against each other. Both of you should get legal advice before agreeing to this.

Where you and your partner own the home jointly both of you have to agree to a sale and the money from the sale is shared between you. If you and your partner cannot agree about whether the home should be sold, an application for sale can be made to the court. In the case of a married couple the court may refuse to order a sale or postpone it. But where the owners are not married a sale will always be ordered.

Where you are living in your partner's home or a jointly owned home you should agree with your partner who is going to pay the running costs (see Chapter 6 for ways of saving tax). If you cannot agree the court can apportion the costs as it thinks fit.

Your partner may not agree to your staying on in the home, perhaps because he or she wants to live there or sell it. See Chapters 2 and 3 for your rights to live there and to exclude your partner. Ways of preventing your partner from selling the home without your agreement are dealt with in Chapter 2. Another method of being able to stay in the home, which is available if you are married and have grounds for divorce (see Chapter 8), is to start divorce proceedings and claim either to have the home made over to you on divorce or to have the right to occupy it after divorce. The court may, however, take the view that it would be better for the home to be sold.

Who owns the savings and investments?

The fact that a bank, building society or similar account is in your name does not necessarily mean you own the money in it; it just means you can withdraw it. Ownership depends on where the money came from and what the intention was in putting it into your account. For example, if only you put your pay or savings in then the money belongs entirely to you. On the other hand, if your partner has put money into your account so that you can pay your partner's business expenses whilst he or she is abroad, then the money belongs to your partner.

The ownership of money in a joint account in names of you and your partner depends on how much each of you contributed and your intentions in opening the joint account. If only you put money in, but you made the account joint so that your partner could sign cheques or withdraw money as well, the money will belong entirely to you. On the other hand if your intention was to pool resources with your partner (which is more likely nowadays), or if both you and your partner put money in, you are both joint owners.

Investments, such as stocks and shares, belong to you if they are in your name. If the certificate is in the name of you and your partner, each of you own an equal half share wherever the money came from.

If you and your partner cannot agree on how to deal with the money (savings and investments) you will have to go to court. This is generally worth doing only if there is a sizeable sum at stake. On divorce the court can divide up the money between you irrespective of actual ownership. The factors that it takes into account in deciding how much (if any) to award are discussed in Chapter 5.

Am I liable for my partner's debts?

The general rule is that you are not liable for your partner's debts, hire purchase or other financial commitments. But you can be made to pay if:

- you agreed to act as guarantor. This means that if your partner whose debts you have guaranteed fails to pay, you will be required to pay instead. It is then up to you to try to get the amount you paid back from your partner.

- you have agreed to be "jointly and severally liable" with your partner. Common examples of joint and several liability are rent due by joint tenants, repayments due on a joint loan, and an overdraft on a joint account. You can be called on to pay the whole amount. If you do pay you are entitled to ask your partner to reimburse you for the half share you have paid on his or her behalf.

- Your partner has not paid his or her share of the council tax bill for any period that you were living together. You can be made to pay the whole amount of the council tax bill. You are entitled to recover your partner's share but this may involve taking him or her to court.

- your partner has not repaid his or her social fund loan. You can be made to pay. The Benefits Agency may deduct the amount at so much a week from your benefit or bring legal proceedings.

- your husband, wife or child (but not cohabiting partner) died without leaving enough to pay for the funeral and the local authority carried out the funeral. They are entitled to recover the cost from you.

- you are living in the matrimonial home and the court has ordered you to pay the building society (or bank) loan instalments due by your absent spouse. This rule applies only to husbands and wives.

- you authorised your partner to buy something on your behalf. As long as it was made clear to the supplier that your partner was only ordering on your behalf, you and not your partner are liable. You may also be liable if you have in the past paid for goods ordered by your partner, even though you did not expressly authorise the present purchase.

If you are a mail order catalogue agent you are not liable for goods supplied to a customer who fails to pay, even if the customer is your partner. Neither are you liable for purchases or cash withdrawals made by your partner with his or her own credit card unless the bank or other account they are charged against is a joint account or one that you have guaranteed. However, you are liable for purchases or cash withdrawals made by your partner on an extra card when you are the main card-holder.

Hire purchase goods

You are only liable to pay for an article on hire purchase or conditional sale agreement if you signed the form as the purchaser (or a joint purchaser) or as guarantor (see p48). Otherwise if your partner fails to keep up the payments for his or her purchases the hire purchase company must sue your partner not you. They are also entitled to repossess the goods but need a court order if more than one-third of the price due has been paid. Until they are repossessed you can carry on using the goods with the agreement of your partner.

If you want to keep the goods you can contact the hire purchase company and get the agreement transferred to your name. When paid for the goods will belong to you, but you become liable to make the payments under the agreement in future and may be sued if you fail to do so. Alternatively, you can simply pay each instalment as it falls due instead of your partner. In this way you will continue to have the use of the goods and not commit yourself to making future payments. But the drawback is when the goods are fully paid for, they will belong to your partner not you.

Fuel bills

Electricity and gas bills are payable by the person who signed the agreement for supply. This is the person to whom the bills are addressed. The fuel company is entitled to disconnect the supply (a charge is made for reconnection) if a bill is not paid, and legal proceedings will be taken against the person to recover the amount due. You should contact the company at once if you find yourself in difficulties.

If the person who signed the agreement has left, ask for the meter to be read and a new supply agreement to be prepared in your name.

If the company are satisfied that your partner has genuinely left you (a letter from your solicitor may help) they will pursue your partner for the unpaid bills rather than disconnect you. You may be able to recover part at least of the money you spent in paying your partner's bills by applying to the court for an order apportioning the bills.

Telephone bill

Telephone bills are payable by the person whose name is on the telephone account. If your partner's name is on the bill and s/he leaves the home without paying the bill you are not legally liable to pay it. However, the telephone company may not be prepared to provide a service until the arrears are paid. You should contact the company to negotiate. If you are dissatisfied with the service you can contact OFTEL in Scotland at:

The Secretary
2 Greenside Lane
Edinburgh
EH1 3AH
Tel.: 0131 244 5576

Who to inform about splitting up

Bank: You should contact your branch if you want to open, close or change the names on an account. It is probably better to close a joint account on splitting up because then your partner will not be able to withdraw money that you put in, and you will not be liable for any overdraft that your partner incurs afterwards.

Inland revenue: If you and your partner are married to each other, you should inform your tax office of any separation since this can alter the way in which you will be taxed in the future. See Chapter 6 for further details.

Landlord: When you and your partner have decided to split up you should contact the landlord either to make arrangements for giving up the tenancy or to see if the non-tenant partner can take over the tenancy. Don't be frightened of contacting the landlord. As long as you are married to the tenant or are a cohabiting partner with occupancy rights the landlord cannot put you out simply because the tenant no longer lives there. You can of course still be evicted (a court order is necessary) if the rent is not paid (see p25).

Mortgage lender: You should contact the building society, bank or other lender if you and your partner plan to alter the ownership of the home between yourselves. In theory lenders can refuse to agree as long as the loan remains outstanding, but in practice they will agree to an alteration, provided they are satisfied the loan instalments will continue to be paid. If you, as new owner, do not have sufficient income, your partner or another person may be asked to act as guarantor. You will need a solicitor to prepare the necessary documents altering the ownership.

See p26 for what to do if your partner stops paying the loan instalments.

Benefits agency: You should inform your local Benefits Agency office of your splitting up if you are receiving any state benefit. The separation will probably affect the rate of benefit or even whether you are still entitled to it. You should tell them promptly because if you are overpaid as a result of not telling them, you will be liable to pay back the extra and may be prosecuted for receiving benefit which you were not entitled to. On the other hand you may become eligible for benefits. See p10 for how to obtain confidential advice.

Council tax: You should contact the local authority if you leave the home. Otherwise you may be pursued for any council tax in respect of the home for which you are jointly responsible.

Credit companies: Where you are jointly liable with your partner for goods bought with a credit card you should think about contacting the credit organisation to see if this agreement can be ended. Otherwise you may be held liable for goods your partner buys after you have split up. See p49 for what to do about hire purchase goods.

Fuel and telephone companies: If the agreement for the supply of electricity, gas or the telephone is in your name you should contact the fuel company or telephone company on moving out. Otherwise you may find yourself having to pay for future supplies used by your partner.

Other tasks to consider

Wills: On splitting up you and your partner should consider making wills or altering your wills.

If you do not leave a will your husband or wife may inherit most of your estate as long as you have not been divorced. On the other hand you may wish to leave something to your former partner whom you were living with but not married to. Unless you make a will he or she will inherit nothing.

You should consider altering your will on splitting up. If you do not cancel bequests to your former partner he or she may still be entitled to them even after divorce. You should see a solicitor about making a new will, but remember that you can't completely disinherit your husband or wife, because as long as you are still married he or she can claim legal rights (see p73).

Nominations: Several organisations, such as friendly societies, allow you to nominate a person to whom the amount in your account or benefits are to be paid on your death. If you have nominated your partner you should, on splitting up, consider whether to cancel the nomination. If you decide to cancel it, you will need to contact the organisation and fill in the appropriate forms.

Life Insurance: Many people have life insurance policies on their own lives in which the benefits are payable to their executors or their partners. In the latter case you should think about whether the policy ought to be changed when you and your partner split up. You should not surrender the policy or stop paying the premiums without first consulting a solicitor or accountant. It may be possible to alter the terms of the policy by agreement. The court on granting a divorce can alter the terms of a life policy as part of the financial settlement.

Similar problems arise when one partner insures the other's life, or when a joint policy is taken out on both lives.

CHAPTER FIVE

FUTURE FINANCES
MONEY FROM YOUR PARTNER

This chapter deals mainly with maintenance from your partner for yourself and any children, and financial arrangements on divorce. A final section contains information on your rights to inherit from your former partner.

Separation

Can I get maintenance for myself?
How to get maintenance
How much maintenance will I get?
Can I get maintenance for the children?
How to get child maintenance
Using the Child Support Agency (CSA)
Calculating child support
Cost of using the Child Support Agency
How child support is paid

Divorce

What can I apply for?
How the court decides what to do
The court's orders

Changes in maintenance

Can the amount be changed?
What happens if the person paying maintenance dies?
What happens if I remarry or cohabit?
What happens if my partner is made bankrupt?

Enforcing your maintenance

Maintenance by court order or by enforceable agreement
Maintenance claimed through the Child Support Agency

Your inheritance rights

Where a will is left
Where no will is left
Survivorship destinations
Your rights under your partner's pension scheme

The type of financial support you can get from your partner for yourself and the children depends on whether or not you have been married and what stage you have reached in splitting up.

If you are married, you and your spouse are liable to maintain each other financially. If you separate, without getting divorced you can make an arrangement, either informally or through the courts to support each other. If you are not married you and your partner do not have any legal obligation to support each other financially while you live together or after you split up.

If you are married you can make further financial arrangements at the point that you get divorced. This could include a lump sum, a transfer of property, regular payments (known as a periodical allowance) as well as maintenance for any children.

All parents are liable to support their children financially, whether or not they are married to each other. This means that if you split up and have the children living with you, your former partner will be liable to contribute towards the children's upkeep, whether or not you were married to each other.

Separation

Can I get maintenance for myself?

If you are married and are separating you and your spouse have a legal obligation to provide for each other as long as you remain married (this is known as aliment). If you and your partner are not married to each other you have no obligation to provide for each other although you may agree to do so.

How to get maintenance

While you and your spouse live together aliment is given by provision of a home, food, clothing and other things suitable to your standard of living.

On separation aliment is usually given entirely in money (so much a week or month). Your spouse could aliment you by providing a home and paying bills for it. You can get aliment for yourself by payments made:

- voluntarily; *or*

- under an enforceable written agreement (an agreement that contains a legally binding obligation to pay aliment), sometimes called a separation agreement; *or*

- under a court order.

The advantages and disadvantages of each method are shown in the accompanying chart.

	Advantages	Disadvantages
Voluntary Payments	Does not count as payee's taxable income Amount payable easily altered. No legal fees.	Not legally enforceable. No tax allowance given to payer. Have to go to court if can't agree how much should be paid.
Enforceable Agreement	Legally enforceable. Agreement may provide for alteration if circumstances change. Tax allowance may be given to payer up to a certain amount (see p84). Cheaper than a court order.	You will have to pay for the legal costs, although you may be entitled to help with these through the legal advice and assistance scheme.
Court Order	Legally enforceable. Tax allowance may be given to payer up to a certain amount. (see p84)	Alterable only by another court order. Only available if legally entitled to aliment. Slower than other methods and may involve publicity. If you are successful your spouse will have to pay your legal expenses as well as the aliment. If you lose you will have to pay your and your spouse's expenses. Legal aid is available. You cannot get aliment for yourself from your cohabiting partner by means of a court order because he or she has no legal obligation to aliment you. Your partner may agree to provide for you voluntarily or sign an enforceable agreement. Your partner does have a legal obligation to support his or her children and any children accepted into the family. (see p54).

How much maintenance will I get?

The amount of aliment payable voluntarily or under an enforceable agreement depends on what was arranged between the parties concerned.

In legal proceedings for aliment the court will award only what is reasonable. It is not possible to give any rule of thumb since what is considered reasonable depends very much on the individual circumstances of each case and the views of the judge hearing it. The main factors taken into account are :-

- the applicant's needs and resources; *and*
- the payer's needs and resources; *and*
- the standard of living previously enjoyed by the applicant; *and*
- the length of the marriage.

Your spouse can defend your claim for aliment on the ground that he or she is willing to have you living with him or her and provide for you in that way. The court will then look at all the circumstances to see whether the offer is reasonable. If the court thinks it is reasonable your claim will be dismissed. It would be unreasonable for you to have to accept your spouse's offer if he or she had committed adultery, behaved violently or unreasonably, or his or her home was not suitable.

Your needs depend to some extent on the standard of living enjoyed when living together. You cannot normally expect to maintain this standard, but you should not be reduced to the "bread line" if you lived well before and your spouse can afford to pay a decent aliment.

Needs are primarily your own needs, but the court *may* take into account the fact that you support other dependants (such as an aged parent or a cohabiting partner) even though you have no legal obligation to do so. Where you have a legal obligation to support (a new child for example) this *must* be taken into account in assessing needs. The amount of maintenance paid for any children will also be taken into account. Your spouse's needs are assessed in the same way. Your and your spouse's resources generally means income but capital may be taken into account. Each of you will have to give evidence of income in the shape of recent pay slips, income tax returns etc. Both of you can be ordered to provide evidence of your resources. If you are living with another partner the court will take that into account, but your new partner cannot be ordered to disclose his or her resources. A woman is unlikely to be awarded aliment for herself if she is living with a new partner.

The past conduct or behaviour of the person claiming aliment is not taken into account in assessing how much to pay, unless it would be quite unjust to ignore it - if you had ill-treated your spouse, for example.

You should try and agree informally with your spouse the amount of aliment. Both of you can then ask the court to award this agreed amount instead of fighting lengthy and expensive legal proceedings. Moreover, an amount which has been agreed is more likely to be paid than one which has been "imposed" by the court.

The court will usually order your spouse to pay a certain sum of aliment (monthly or weekly) starting from the date of making the order. You can ask the court to backdate the order to when you started proceedings or even earlier, but in the latter case, you must have a very good reason - your spouse had left and you had only just traced him or her, for example.

The court proceedings for aliment will take some months. During this period you can apply for interim aliment which is assessed on a fairly rough and ready basis. Interim aliment comes to an end when the court decides your aliment claim.

Can I get maintenance for the children?

Your spouse or cohabiting partner has a legal obligation to maintain his or her own children (including adopted children) and any child accepted as a child of the family (such as a child of yours by a previous marriage). A child who is being fostered is not counted as being accepted as a child of the family.

The liability to maintain a child lasts until the child is 18. An obligation also exists to maintain older children up to the age of 25 if they are in further education or training, for example, they are at university or college or being trained for a trade or profession.

How to get child maintenance

While you and your partner and the children live together as a family, the children are maintained by the provision of home, food, clothing and other things. On separation the absent parent usually gives money to the parent with care of the children to help support them. It is usually the parent with care of the children who claims maintenance on their behalf. Children over 12 can claim maintenance in their own right though this has tax disadvantages (see p85).

You can reach a voluntary or legally enforceable agreement with the absent parent as to how much maintenance should be paid for the children. The Child Support Agency (CSA) deals with most types of maintenance for children, instead of the courts. Any agreement cannot prevent you applying to the CSA for child support so the agreed maintenance should be in line with what the CSA would award.

The CSA deals with day to day costs of child maintenance for children who are:-

- under 16; *or*

- under 19 and still in full-time secondary education; *or*

- 16 or 17 and registered for work or youth training but have not actually started.

Using the Child Support Agency (CSA)

You may be forced to use the CSA if you claim Income Support, Income-related Jobseeker's Allowance, Family Credit or Disability Working Allowance for yourself and the children. In these cases you will be required to apply for child support as a condition of getting full benefit.

The risk of harm or undue distress

You may not wish the CSA to pursue the absent parent for maintenance because of the risk of harm or distress to yourself and the children. If this is the case you should sign and return the 'letter of declaration' accompanying the maintenance application form but should not sign the form as this gives the CSA authorisation to make investigations. A Child Support Officer will want to interview you about your fears but you can ask for a home interview and a friend or adviser can be present. There is no legal requirement to attend an interview and you could send a letter setting out the reasons why you do not want to co-operate. However it may be difficult to convince the CSA that there is a risk if you are not interviewed.

Your fears about threats of violence, abuse or verbal intimidation or threats to demand greater contact with the children or take them away should be taken seriously. The CSA may well decide not to pursue the absent parent for maintenance if he has a history of violence or abuse.

If you do not want to co-operate because you want to sever links with the absent parent or you do not want the children to see him or her this will not be accepted as a reason in itself for not cooperating as the CSA is not supposed to pass on your address.

If you refuse to authorise the CSA to pursue your partner for maintenance and it judges that you do not have good reason to do so, it may direct that your income support be reduced (see chapter 6) but it cannot pursue the absent parent without your authorisation.

Calculating child support

Child support is calculated by applying a fixed formula. There are certain standard allowances and the sum payable is also related to the incomes of the parents involved. The aim of the legislation is that children are entitled to share in the lifestyle they would have enjoyed had their parents been living together.

When calculating child support, no account will be taken of the past conduct or behaviour of the parent with care of the children. It does not matter who is "responsible" for the relationship breaking down. The contributions of the parents are decided in relation to the size of their individual incomes and their needs.

Departures: A degree of flexibility is built into the system which allows "departures" from the standard calculation in certain specific circumstances. These include when a parent has expenses which have not been taken into account, such as:-

- costs of keeping in contact with the children;

- costs of supporting a step child in a "second family";

- travel-to-work costs which have not already been taken into account;

- costs of long-term illness or disability of the parent or another dependant;

- debts incurred before separation;

- financial commitments made before 1993 which would be difficult to withdraw from.

A departure can also be made where one parent considers that the other parent's lifestyle is not consistent with the declared income, or the parent's new partner ought to be contributing to the costs of housing.

Appeals: If one of the parties is unhappy with the figure resulting from the Child Support calculation they may seek a review from the CSA. If they are unhappy with this review they may appeal to the Child Support Appeal Tribunal. The Tribunal may however only look at whether the rules have been applied correctly. It cannot examine matters such as additional expenses which are not covered in the legislation.

Cost of using the Child Support Agency

If the CSA makes a maintenance assessment, whether or not a parent has chosen to use it, each parent will have to pay a fee to the CSA unless they are on Income Support, Income-based Jobseeker's Allowance, Family Credit or Disability Working Allowance or on a low income. The CSA may charge a fee to the parent with care for the collection of any maintenance assessed.

How child support is paid

Maintenance assessed by the CSA can be paid in two ways. The CSA should ask both parents how they would prefer to make or receive payments. If the parents cannot agree then the CSA will decide.

The absent parent can either pay the maintenance direct to the parent with care or pay it to the CSA which will then pass it on to the parent with care.

If the parent with care is on Income Support, it may be to her or his advantage to have the CSA collect the maintenance payments. The parent with care will then receive a fixed amount each week made up of a mixture of child maintenance and Income Support. If a maintenance payment is missed, the amount of the payment will stay the same but will be made up of Income Support only. If the missing maintenance payment is then recovered by the CSA, the CSA will keep it. If the absent parent is making maintenance payments direct to the parent with care, however, and a payment is missed the parent with care will have to inform the CSA. The CSA will inform the Benefits Agency so that the difference is made up in Income Support but there is no "fast track" process for this.

In the following cases child maintenance is still dealt with by the courts:-

Your partner has accepted a child into the family

The CSA does not deal with maintenance for stepchildren. However if your partner has taken on a parental role towards a child or children and treated them as part of his or her family then he or she can be asked to provide financially for them. When the court is considering a case of this kind it will take into account any contribution to the child's maintenance which is, or should be, provided by someone else. If the child's father or mother is also liable for maintenance the court would take this into account in fixing your partner's level of payments.

Not habitually resident in the UK

If either parent or the children are not habitually resident in the UK, child maintenance will be dealt with by the courts. Someone who is working abroad for a fixed period or who works abroad but frequently returns and has a home in the UK would probably still qualify as habitually resident in the UK. However, someone who has moved abroad with no plans to return to the UK, or who has gone to live in a country where they have family ties or who has a series of fixed term contracts abroad and rarely or never comes back to the UK might not.

School fees

If your children are at a private school, the CSA will not take account of this in its calculations. You will have to ask the court to make an order for school fees if you cannot come to an agreement with the absent parent.

Expenses needed to help with a child's disability

Extra costs because a child is disabled, for example, the cost of a wheelchair, special adaptations are not taken into account by the CSA. They can be fixed by the courts if you can't reach an agreement with the absent parent.

Top up maintenance

The CSA formula has a ceiling for maximum maintenance. If the absent parent is on a very high income and you feel that the amount the CSA proposes does not reflect the resources available for maintenance, it is possible to apply to the court for additional maintenance payments.

16 and 17 year olds

You may have children who are 16 or 17 but cannot apply for maintenance through the CSA because they are not in full-time non-advanced education or registered for work or youth training. In this case you can apply to the courts for maintenance for them.

Children 18 or over and under 25

Children aged 18 or over but under 25 can claim aliment from their parents if they are in full-time further education or training. The education or training must be reasonable and appropriate. It would probably be reasonable for a child to go to university if they had the appropriate academic qualifications but the courts might not expect parents to fund a series of higher degrees after this.

Pre-April 1993 agreements or court orders

If you have an agreement or court order for maintenance from before April 1993 you cannot apply to the Child Support Agency unless you have started to claim Income Support, Income related Jobseeker's Allowance, Family Credit or Disability Working Allowance. You have to enforce the agreement or order. The courts can also vary the amounts payable.

Divorce

If separation is followed by divorce, the court considers what new financial arrangements should be made. This is discussed in the following section.

What can I apply for?

When the court grants a decree of divorce it can make a variety of orders adjusting the financial position of you and your spouse. These orders are called financial provision orders. The main orders are:

- ordering you or your spouse to pay a lump sum (called a "capital sum") to the other;
- ordering you or your spouse to pay the other a periodical allowance.

This is a regular sum usually ordered to be paid weekly or monthly.

The court can no longer make orders for child maintenance (except in certain cases see p62) as this is dealt with by the CSA. However other orders that can be made include a transfer of the tenancy of the home, transfer of the ownership of the home or other property, regulating the occupation of the home and a pension order. Either you or your spouse can apply for an order or orders; it doesn't matter which of you brings the divorce proceedings.

You and your spouse should try to agree how the assets are to be divided and what payments are to be paid, and then ask the court to make the appropriate orders. Be flexible and reasonable. Don't make inflated claims or regard certain matters as non–negotiable otherwise you may have to pay all the legal costs.

An agreed settlement is more likely to be implemented, whereas court orders granted after bitter wrangles may well turn out to be unenforceable. As child maintenance paid under the Child Support Act contains an amount for the parent looking after the children, your partner may be unwilling to pay you a periodical allowance. Mediation services are available to help couples to reach agreement about their finances and arrangements for the children (see p7–11 for further details).

How the court decides what to do

The following principles guide the court in making financial orders:

- Family assets should be shared fairly between you and your spouse; *and*

- account should be taken of economic advantages you derived from contributions made by your spouse, and economic disadvantages you suffered in the interest of your spouse or the family; *and*

- the future child care burden should be shared fairly between you and your spouse; *and*

- where you or your spouse has been financially dependant on the other during the marriage, support should be provided for up to three years; *and*

- when divorce will cause serious financial hardship to you or your spouse, provision should be made for a reasonable period.

Your or your spouse's conduct will not be taken into account in relation to the first three principles. It will be taken into account for the last 2 principles only if it was so bad it would be quite unjust to ignore it.

Sharing family assets: These are to be shared equally unless there is a special reason for doing otherwise. Some examples of where an unequal division might be made are where the assets were bought with your or your family's money, or where your spouse has a business (a farm for example) which cannot be divided and if sold would deprive him or her of a livelihood.

Family assets mean all the property and belongings you or your spouse acquired during your marriage unless given by another person or inherited.

They include items such as the home, its contents, savings and investments, life policies, and rights under an occupational or private pension scheme (very important in the case of elderly couples (see p74). Assets you and your spouse acquired before marriage are not regarded as family assets. The only exceptions to this rule are the home and its contents. In so far as any of these items were bought before marriage for use by both of you after marriage they are treated as family assets.

Economic advantages and disadvantages: You will be entitled to have taken into account your contributions which have increased your spouse's wealth. Your contributions may be financial or non-financial. For example you may have helped him or her build up the business, you may have worked to enable him or her to be trained, or you may have paid some of the bills for the home, done repairs or improvements or kept house. Your spouse's contributions to your wealth are also taken into account.

Any economic disadvantages either of you suffered in the interest of the other or the family are also to be taken into account. For example, you may have given up your career in order to stay at home and look after the children, or your spouse may not have taken a better job because you did not want to move away from your job.

Sharing child care burden: This can be useful where there are costs over and above maintenance for the children. The parent looking after them having to buy a larger house is an example.

Financial dependency: If you have been financially dependant on your spouse you will be entitled to some financial provision to cushion you from the loss of this support after divorce. This support lasts for up to three years from the date of the divorce only, since it is designed to give you time to find a job or get training so you can support yourself.

Severe financial hardship: Even where all the above factors have been taken into account you may be severely affected financially by divorce. For example, if you are an elderly woman who has never worked during a long marriage you will be entitled to financial provision for a reasonable period, the rest of your life perhaps. In assessing how much you need, the court looks at your age, health, earning capacity, how long you have been married and what standard of living you have enjoyed.

The court's orders

On the basis of these principles the court makes an order or orders for your financial provision. It must first consider whether it is possible for your spouse to provide for you solely by means of a lump sum and/or a transfer of property. For example, if you have no children the court may think that a modest lump sum to support you until you get back into employment, plus one half of the family assets would be sufficient. But if you are elderly and unable to support yourself your provision will have to last for several years and your spouse may not be able to afford to pay this in a lump sum.

Only if a lump sum and/or a transfer of property will not provide for you sufficiently can the court make a periodical allowance. Furthermore, you have to demonstrate that a periodical allowance is justified on the grounds of fair sharing of child caring costs, or financial dependency or severe economic hardship (see p65). Your periodical allowance may be payable for an indefinite period, for a fixed number of years or until a specified event happens – the children leave home, for example. Most people want to make a clean financial break from their ex-spouses, and periodical allowances are uncommon. You must apply for a lump sum or transfer of property order in the divorce proceedings; afterwards is too late. The lump sum can be ordered to be paid in instalments, or payment of it can be postponed. Similarly the date of transfer of property can be postponed. This could be useful where the property belongs to a spouse who uses it for business. The transfer could be delayed until he or she retires.

If you are legally aided the Legal Aid Charge may mean you get a lot less than the court awarded you. See p114 for further details.

Changes in maintenance

Can the amount be changed?

Voluntary payments: If your (ex)spouse/partner is supporting you and/or the children by voluntary payments he or she can change the amount payable at any time. You would have to take legal proceedings for aliment (but see p55) or go to the CSA for child maintenance (see p58) if he or she refused to pay the amount you think should be being paid.

Payments under enforceable agreements: Enforceable agreements may provide for a change in the amount payable when circumstances change. The amount may, for instance, be calculated by reference to your and your (ex)spouse's/partner's incomes, so that if you get an increase it will go down, but if he or she gets an increase it will go up. The amount may also increase as the children grow older.

What can you do if you are dissatisfied with the amount under the agreement and you cannot reach a new agreement with the payer depends on the type of maintenance involved.

Your aliment: You can apply to the court unless the agreement prohibits this. Even then the court will allow an application if the agreement was not fair and reasonable when it was made.

Your periodical allowance: You can apply to the court only if the agreement expressly allows this.

Children's aliment: You can apply only if the agreement was made before April 1993. The court is very unlikely to uphold a clause prohibiting an application and will not be bound by any method in the agreement for variation. With a post April 1993 agreement you have to apply to the CSA.

Court orders: If there has been a change in circumstances since the court awarded you aliment, either you or your (ex)spouse/partner can go back to the court to ask for the amount to be varied.

For example if:

- he or she gets a better job; *or*

- you lose your job or become part-time; *or*

- you have additional dependants (such as other children) to support.

On the other hand if:

- you get a better job; *or*

- he or she becomes unemployed; *or*

- he or she has additional dependants (such as a new partner) to support; *or*

- you are being supported by a new partner (see p69) your aliment could be decreased, terminated or continued only for a limited period.

Inflation by itself may not justify an increase. The court would have to be satisfied that your (ex)spouse/partner could afford to pay more since s/he would feel the effects of inflation too. The court can backdate any variation to the date of the application or even to the date when the circumstances changed.

Your periodical allowance can be varied similarly. In addition, the court can, if asked, cancel your allowance and substitute an order requiring your ex-spouse to pay you a lump sum and/or to transfer property to you. You might find this useful if your ex-spouse is not paying your periodical allowance regularly. Your ex-spouse might prefer to pay you a lump sum (by instalments perhaps) rather than an allowance which could last for the remainder of your life. You should think carefully about substitution, however, because your ex-spouse's income (and hence your periodical allowance) might well increase over the years. Once the court has made the substitution it cannot be changed back again.

Lump sum and transfer of property orders: Once these orders have been made they cannot normally be changed. All the court can do, if asked, is to alter the date of payment or transfer. For example, if your ex-spouse was ordered to pay you a lump sum, say one month after divorce, he or she could apply to pay it by instalments spread over a year or so. On the other hand if he was originally allowed to pay by instalments, you could ask the court to speed up the instalments or order that the outstanding balance be paid immediately. Similarly, either of you could ask the court to vary the date when an item of property is to be transferred.

The court can cancel or vary a lump sum or transfer of property order on bankruptcy. If your ex-husband or wife:

- is made bankrupt within 5 years after the court order was made; *and*

- the order made him or her insolvent - debts exceeded remaining assets.

The court may order you to repay or return all or part of the money or property. This is likely to be very uncommon. The divorce court is usually aware of a couple's financial circumstances and so would not have granted a lump sum or transfer of property order which made your ex-husband or wife insolvent.

Child support: If there is a change of circumstances, either the parent with care or the absent parent can apply for the amount of child support to be reviewed. A change of circumstances might include a reduction or increase in income or either parent having another child. If an error is discovered there will also be a review.

The maintenance assessment will otherwise be reviewed on an annual basis. Reviews are carried out by a Child Support Officer who will give parents 14 days notice that the review will take place. Both parents will be asked to fill in a review form to give up to date information about their income and obligations (unless they are on Income Support).

What happens if the person paying maintenance dies?

Aliment and maintenance: Your aliment and the children's maintenance comes to an end automatically if the person paying maintenance dies. Any arrears which were owing at the date of death have to be paid out of his or her estate (money and property left by him or her). You should tell the executors of the estate about your claim for arrears as soon as you can.

It is possible to apply to the court for an order requiring your late partner's executors to make an allowance out of the estate to replace your aliment and/or the children's maintenance. But these applications are most unusual as they are only possible if your partner left a great deal of money and you and/or the children did not get much under your partner's will or by way of legal rights (see p72–/3).

Periodical allowance: Your periodical allowance, on the other hand, continues even after your ex-spouse dies. The executors must continue to pay your allowance out of the estate and you can claim any arrears out of the estate. But the executors can (and will) apply to the court for an order cancelling your allowance (and the cancellation can be backdated). Normally this will be granted unless your ex-spouse died well off and you are in need of further support.

What happens if I remarry or cohabit?

If you live with another partner your aliment or periodical allowance does not come to an end automatically. But your (ex)spouse can apply to the court for it to be decreased or cancelled. Normally it will be cancelled if you are living with another partner whether or not he or she is supporting you. But this is a "grey area" and practice varies.

If you remarry after divorce any periodical allowance payable ceases automatically. Your ex-spouse remains liable to pay you any arrears which were owing at the date of your remarriage. You should tell your ex-spouse of your remarriage as soon as it takes place, otherwise you may be faced with having to repay the instalments you received after remarriage in a lump sum.

If you remarry or live with another partner this does not usually make any difference to the amount of aliment that your ex-partner must pay for his or her children. It may make some difference to the amount of child maintenance assessed by the CSA.

What happens if my partner is made bankrupt?

If your (ex)spouse or partner was paying aliment or periodical allowance and is made bankrupt you can put in a claim for any arrears which were unpaid at the date of bankruptcy. You should notify your claim to the trustee who is appointed to sell the bankrupt's property for the benefit of all of his or her creditors including you. You will probably be paid only a proportion of your claim; the remainder is written off.

The bankruptcy does not automatically terminate your aliment or periodical allowance or the children's maintenance. However, the court, on application by your (ex)spouse or partner, can cancel or reduce your aliment or periodical allowance and the CSA can reduce child maintenance payments. Until these changes are made, maintenance is still due for the period after the start of the bankruptcy. See p68 for the effect of bankruptcy on lump sum or transfer of property orders.

Enforcing your maintenance

Maintenance by court order or enforceable agreement

Aliment and periodical allowance are notoriously difficult to enforce because many people become reluctant payers once their relationships with their former families have cooled. Payments under an agreement tend to be kept up. Even if you know where your (ex)spouse or partner is, the legal methods of enforcing payment (called diligence) are not very effective unless he or she is in steady employment or owns property or goods which can be sold. The Benefits Agency may be able to help in tracing him or her. Ask your solicitor to contact them if you wish to make use of their services.

If your aliment or periodical allowance is contained in a court order or legally enforceable agreement and has not been paid you can:

- negotiate a payment plan with your (ex)spouse/partner; *or*

- claim social security benefits (see Ch6); *or*

- use the legal methods of enforcing payment.

If you and your (ex)spouse/partner are on reasonable terms with each other, you may be able to reach an agreement that the arrears are to be paid off by instalments in addition to regular payments of maintenance in future. If he or she has a bank account you can suggest that he or she should arrange for the payments to be made by standing order to ensure regularity.

If your total income including your aliment or periodical allowance is less than your Income Support entitlement, you should claim. The Benefits Agency will take steps to recover from your partner the amount of money they have paid in benefit to you (except benefit paid for yourself after divorce). See p78–80 for further details. If you have children and you are not using the CSA to claim maintenance for them, you may be required to do so if you claim Income Support (see p59).

If your partner is employed you can use a current maintenance arrestment on his or her pay. The employer will deduct your maintenance from his or her pay when each instalment is due and send it to you. Other enforcement procedures you can use are arrestment of your partner's bank or building society account, poinding and warrant sale of his or her goods, and civil imprisonment (aliment only not periodical allowance). These other procedures only recover arrears of maintenance due at the date when diligence was done, although the threat of repetition may ensure that you are paid regularly in future.

You will need a solicitor for diligence. If you were legally aided when you applied for the court order, your existing legal aid certificate covers the costs of diligence (except civil imprisonment) for up to 12 months after the date of the court order. After this you will have to apply for fresh legal aid (see Appendix 1). Civil imprisonment always requires a separate legal aid application.

You may be using the CSA to claim maintenance but also claiming maintenance through the courts for children's expenses which fall outwith the remit of the CSA (for example, for stepchildren). If this is the case you can ask the CSA to collect both types of maintenance. The CSA will not collect or enforce your aliment or periodical allowance.

If your partner lives in another part of the United Kingdom, a European Union country or certain other foreign countries, the courts there will help in enforcing payments due under your Scottish court order. You will need to get your solicitor in Scotland to take the appropriate action on your behalf.

Maintenance claimed through the Child Support Agency

If you have been assessed by the CSA you will be receiving maintenance for the children either by direct payment from the absent parent or the absent parent will be paying maintenance to the CSA and they will be passing it on to you.

If the absent parent is paying you direct and misses a payment, you should consider contacting the CSA and asking to use its collection service. It is important to do this promptly as the CSA will not pursue arrears of maintenance until the collection service is requested. You should keep your own record so that you can show that payments have not been made.

The CSA will send the absent parent an arrears notice showing the amount owed and requesting payment. He or she can then agree a payment plan with the CSA to pay outstanding arrears.

If maintenance is still not paid, the CSA can make a deduction from earning order (DEO). This means that the amount owed will be deducted from the absent parent's pay by his or her employer. A DEO cannot leave him or her with less than the exempt income to live on.

If a DEO would be inappropriate because, for example, the absent parent is not employed, the CSA can use diligences to enforce payment such as arrestment of his/her bank or building society account, poinding and warrant sale of goods and civil imprisonment.

Your inheritance rights

Your inheritance rights on the death of your former partner depend on whether you were married to him or her and whether he or she left a will.

Where a will is left

If you and your partner are not married to each other you will inherit only what your partner leaves you by will or under a survivorship destination (see p74).

If you and your husband or wife are still married to each other you are entitled to whatever he or she left you in the will or under a survivorship destination. If the will leaves you nothing or only a small legacy you can claim "legal rights". Legal rights amount to half of your late husband's or wife's moveable property (roughly everything except buildings and land) if there are no children or descendants surviving, or one third if there are. You have to choose between what (if anything) you are left in the will and your legal rights - you cannot have both.

If you are divorced you cannot claim legal rights from your ex-husband or wife. If he or she did not alter the will after divorce you may still be entitled to any legacy left to you, especially if you have been named rather than been described simply as "my wife" or "my husband". The law here is rather complex and you should seek independent legal advice if you think you have a claim.

Where no will is left

If you were never married or are divorced, you are entitled to nothing if your partner or (ex)husband or wife does not leave a will. But if you are still married when your husband or wife dies, you could end up inheriting most of his or her estate. A husband who is judicially separated from his wife does not inherit any unwilled property she acquired after separation.

First, you are entitled to the house (or share of the house) owned by your late husband or wife if:

- you were living in it when he or she died; *and*

- it (or the share of it) is not worth more than £110,000; *and*

- it is in Scotland; *and*

- there is no survivorship destination (see below).

Where the house (or share of it) is worth more than £110,000 you get £110,000 in cash instead. But you may be able to buy the house from the estate by making up the difference yourself. You may only get the value (up to £110,000) if the house forms part of a larger property used for business purposes - a farmhouse on a farm for example.

You will normally be entitled to take over your late husband's or wife's tenancy if you were living in the house before the death. You should contact the landlord as soon as possible to let them know what you intend to do.

Secondly, you get the furniture and contents owned by your late husband or wife up to £20,000 in value and a cash sum of up to either £30,000 or £50,000. The larger sum is due if your late husband or wife leaves no surviving children or descendants.

Thirdly, you get one third of any remaining moveable property (roughly everything except buildings and land) if your late husband or wife leaves children or other descendants. If there are no children or descendants surviving you get one half.

Finally, if your late husband or wife is not survived by any descendants, brothers/sisters or their descendants, or parents, you will inherit the whole of the estate.

Survivorship destinations

When a couple buy a home together the title is frequently taken in such a way that the whole property passes to the survivor on the death of one of the couple. In this case you will inherit the home on your partner's death as long as:

- the title has not been altered after you separated or divorced; *and*

- your partner has not left his or her share to someone else by will.

Whether your partner is entitled to leave his or her share by will to someone else depends on how the home was paid for. Generally, if you helped pay for the home your partner cannot leave his or her share by will to someone else.

Your rights under your partner's pension scheme

Private pension schemes for employed or self-employed people generally provide for a pension to be paid to widows. Many schemes now also provide for pensions to widowers especially if they were financially dependant on their wives. Schemes do not normally provide for a pension to be paid to an unmarried partner, but you may be able to make a claim if you are looking after your late partner's children, so it is always worth getting into contact with the managers of the scheme.

Many pension schemes for employed people provide for a lump sum to be paid to the scheme member's estate if he or she dies before retirement. Rather than have this sum form part of the estate, some schemes allow a member to nominate who is to receive it on his or her death. The usual person nominated is a wife or husband and in this case the nomination is automatically cancelled by divorce. If you are not married you could consider asking the managers of the scheme whether your partner can nominate you. In the absence of a nomination the managers can choose. They will normally select the widow(er) or surviving partner.

These rights to a dependant's pension and/or a lump sum can be very valuable especially in the case of elderly people. You will lose your rights to both on divorce, so you should make sure that your loss of these future rights is taken into account in your divorce settlement. See p110 for how divorce can affect your state retirement pension.

On divorce your and your spouse's pension rights form part of the family assets that are to be shared fairly (see p63). The pension rights are valued at the date of separation. The managers of the pension scheme will provide a value or an actuary may be used (this is more expensive). Where the pension scheme was entered before marriage only a proportion based on years of marriage are taken into account. A financial settlement often arrived at is for one partner to keep the pension rights in return for the other becoming the sole owner of the family home.

CHAPTER SIX

MONEY
AND THE STATE

This chapter looks at the various state welfare benefits to which you may be entitled after splitting up and how your and your partner's incomes are taxed then.

Welfare benefits

Income Support
Jobseeker's Allowance
Social fund payments
Family Credit
Housing Benefit
Council Tax Benefit
Child Benefit
Education benefits
National Health Service benefits

Income tax

How splitting up affects your income tax
How maintenance is taxed
Tax relief on home loans
Capital gains tax

Welfare benefits

This book gives brief details of the benefits available at the date of publication. You should check the current position with your local Citizens Advice Bureau or Benefits Agency office.

Income support

This is the main benefit for people with little or no money of their own. It is means tested, so you will only get it if your income and savings are below certain amounts. These amounts change every year and depend upon your circumstances.

You cannot claim Income Support if you work for more than 16 hours a week, or if your partner works for more than 24 hours a week, but you may be able to claim Family Credit instead (see p81).

You can only claim Income Support if you do not have to be available for work. People who usually do not have to be available for work are:

- single parents;

- carers of people with disabilities;

- people over 60;

- people who are unable to work because they are sick or disabled;

- women who are pregnant (from 11 weeks before the baby is due) or who have just had a baby (up to 7 weeks after the baby is born).

These rules may change from time to time so you should get advice about whether you qualify.

If you are not in one of these groups, you are considered to be available for work and hence ineligible for Income Support, but you may be able to claim Jobseeker's Allowance instead. (see p78).

You cannot claim Income Support if you have more than £8,000 in savings (1997/8 figure). Savings include cash, money in a bank or building society account, national savings certificates, unit-trusts, stocks and shares. The value of your home is not counted as savings while you are living there. If you leave the home because you have split up with your partner its value will be ignored for six months. Cash from the sale of your previous home is not counted as savings for six months as long as you are going to use it to buy a new home. These six month periods can be extended if selling, buying or reaching an agreement with your partner about the home proves difficult.

Your furniture and personal possessions do not count as savings unless you have particularly valuable items. The value of any life policy which can be given up for cash is also disregarded.

The way in which a lump sum payable on divorce or arrears of maintenance paid in a lump sum is treated is complex. Depending on the circumstances it may be treated as savings or as income spread out over a number of weeks.

If you have savings of between £3,000 and £8,000 you will be treated as having an income from your savings of £1 per week for every £250 (or amount up to £250) of savings above £3,000.

Income Support is a "passport" to other benefits. You qualify for free school meals, free dental care, free prescriptions, free NHS sight test and money off vouchers for glasses, free NHS wigs, free NHS fabric supports, help with the cost of travelling to hospital for NHS treatment and maximum Housing Benefit.

If you remarry or start living with a new partner your entitlement to Income Support will be reassessed by the Benefits Agency. Living with a new partner will usually affect your (and your partner's) entitlement because for the purposes of claiming Income Support the Benefits Agency has to decide whether or not to treat two people living together as a couple. The amount of Income Support and other benefits to which you were previously entitled will change if you are assessed as living as 'husband and wife' with your new partner. Seek further advice if you are unsure of your position.

How to claim

You claim by filling in a form which you get from your local Benefits Agency office. Usually your claim is dealt with by post, but you may be interviewed to get full details of your financial position. You must not make false statements in order to get Income Support. If you are found out you will have to repay it and may be prosecuted as well.

Jobseeker's Allowance

If you are unemployed and are available for work you may be able to claim Jobseeker's Allowance instead of Income Support. You will have to 'sign on' at your local job centre. The rules for working out how much Income-based Jobseeker's Allowance you can get are similar to those for Income Support. The amount you get depends on your savings and any other income that you have (see p77).

How maintenance affects your Income Support or Income-based Jobseeker's Allowance

Any maintenance payments you and/or the children living with you receive counts as income in working out how much Income Support or Income-based Jobseeker's Allowance you are due. You should contact your local Benefits Agency office promptly if your maintenance stops or is delayed, so that your benefit can be adjusted.

If payments for the children have been assessed and arranged by the Child Support Agency you should inform it if a maintenance payment does not arrive and it will inform the Benefits Agency who will adjust your benefit payments. There is no "fast track" process for this. If the maintenance for the children is regularly late or unpaid you should apply to have it collected by the Child Support Agency. This will ensure that you receive the same amount every week made up of a mixture of child maintenance and or Income Support or Income-based Jobseeker's Allowance. If your partner misses a maintenance payment the amount will not change. The Child Support Agency will pursue your partner for the missing maintenance which it will then keep.

If aliment for a wife or husband is paid irregularly the Benefits Agency may.

- pay you Income Support or Income-based Jobseeker's Allowance regularly as if no maintenance was payable.

  You will have to hand over any maintenance you actually receive;
  or

- make you claim Income Support or Income-based Jobseeker's Allowance every week. The amount you get each week will depend on whether or not maintenance was paid.

It may be difficult to persuade the Benefits Agency to accept the first arrangement as the majority of work collecting maintenance has now been passed to the Child Support Agency.

You are not obliged to take legal proceedings to get maintenance or to enforce the court order you have got before you can claim Income Support. The Benefits Agency will suggest that you take action, but they are not entitled to refuse Income Support or Income-based Jobseeker's Allowance if you say no. You should appeal at once if Income Support or Income-based Jobseeker's Allowance is refused on this ground.

For Income Support or Income-based Jobseeker's Allowance purposes a husband and wife are equally liable to maintain each other and both parents are equally liable to maintain their children. These people are called 'liable relatives'. Neither cohabiting partners nor divorced husbands or wives are liable to maintain each other although if a court order is made on divorce for one partner to pay maintenance to the other this must be paid.

If you claim Income Support or Income-based Jobseeker's Allowance after splitting up, you will be asked for details of any relative liable to maintain you or any children for whom you are claiming (your husband or the children's father, for instance). If you have children and are the parent with care, you will be asked to authorise the Child Support Agency to contact the children's father in order to make a maintenance assessment. You can refuse to authorise this on the grounds of 'undue harm and distress' to yourself and your children (see p59). If the Child Support Agency decides that you do not have a good reason for refusing to cooperate your benefit may be cut.

In the case of aliment for a wife or husband the Benefits Agency will contact any 'liable relative' in order to investigate his or her financial position. If they think that he or she should be paying maintenance or more maintenance, they will request him or her to do so. A liable relative who refuses may be prosecuted and, on being found guilty, fined or imprisoned. Alternatively the Benefits Agency may apply to the court for an order requiring the liable relative to pay them such a sum as the court thinks reasonable.

Social fund payments

These may be made to meet expenses which you cannot otherwise afford. There are 6 different types of payments:

- Maternity payments (£100 in 1997/8). For people on Income Support, Income-based Jobseeker's Allowance, Family Credit or Disability Working Allowance (or who successfully claim within the period shown below) to meet the cost of a cot, pram etc for a new baby. You can claim any time from the 29th week of pregnancy to three months after the birth.

- Funeral payments. For people on Income Support, Income-based Jobseeker's Allowance, Family Credit, Disability Working Allowance, Housing Benefit or Council Tax Benefit to meet the cost of a funeral for someone who died without enough money to pay for a funeral.

These two payments are not subject to the local Benefits Agency office's cash limits. Maternity payments do not have to be repaid, but the Benefits Agency can recover a funeral payment from any money or property left by the dead person.

- Community care grants. For people on Income Support or Income-based Jobseeker's Allowance. Grants may be made to improve claimants' homes to avoid them going into care, or to alleviate long term illness or family breakdown. You do not have to repay a grant. Grants are "cash limited" so that your chance of getting one depends on whether the local Benefits Agency office has any grant money left.

- Budgeting loans. For people who have been on Income Support or Income-based Jobseeker's Allowance for 26 weeks or more. Budgeting loans can be used to help pay for items which cannot be met out of weekly income (such as a new cooker or repairing a leaking roof). These loans are repayable by deduction from future Income Support or Income-based Jobseeker's Allowance payments. They are also cash limited.

- Crisis loans. For anybody who needs money to cope in an emergency, a fire or burglary in your home for example. The loan must be the only way to avoid serious damage or serious risk to the health or safety of you and your dependents. These loans must be repaid and are cash limited.

- Cold weather payments. Income support or Income-based Jobseeker's allowance recipients may receive extra payment (a single sum of £8.50 from November 1997) for any period of 7 consecutive days when the temperature was or is forecast to be 0 degrees centigrade or below, to help with heating costs. You do not have to make a separate claim for this as the Benefits Agency usually pay it automatically.

For all Social Fund payments(apart from cold weather payments). If you and/or your partner have more than £500 in savings the payments will be reduced by the amount you have over £500. This may mean it is not worth your claiming.

Family Credit

Family Credit is a benefit to boost the income of low paid full-time workers who are bringing up at least one dependant child. Full time means 16 hours a week or more.

The amount you will get depends on your income and savings and the number and ages of the children. If you are living with a partner his or her income and savings are added to yours to see whether you qualify. The rules for savings are the same as for Income Support (see p77).

Once Family Credit is awarded it stays at the same rate for 26 weeks even if your circumstances change. Family Credit is tax free. It is worthwhile claiming even if the amount you get is small as your family will get free prescriptions, free dental treatment, free NHS sight test and money off vouchers for glasses, free NHS wigs, free fabric supports and help with the cost of travelling to hospital for NHS treatment (but not free school meals for the children).

Housing Benefit

Housing Benefit helps you to pay housing costs. It covers rent and some other services. It is means tested so that the amount of benefit (if any) you get depends on your income and savings. The rules for savings are the same as Income Support (see p77) except that the upper limit is £16,000. If you are living with your partner his or her income and savings are counted in with yours in working out your entitlement to benefit. The amount of benefit may be affected if there are other people living in the house not dependant on you (for example grown up children, other relatives) because they can be expected to contribute to the rent. Your local authority will advise you.

When you apply for Income Support or Income-based Jobseeker's Allowance you will be given an initial application for Housing Benefit with your form. Your council will then send you another form asking for further details about your rent. If you are not claiming Income Support or Income-based Jobseeker's Allowance you should contact your local authority direct for a claim form.

Council Tax Benefit

Council Tax Benefit (also known as Council Tax Rebate) helps you to pay your Council Tax. It is dealt with by the local authority. You can claim Council Tax Benefit if your income is low enough and your savings are not more than £16,000 (as for Housing Benefit). Alternatively you can claim a rebate called second adult rebate if you have certain other adults living with you who are on a low income.

If you are the only adult in the home, or other adults fall into certain categories, you will qualify for a 25% single person's discount. This is not means tested. Contact your local authority for details.

If you separate it is important to inform all the offices you deal with of your change of circumstances. This may mean telling the Benefits Agency (for Income Support), and the council (for Housing Benefit or Council Tax Benefit).

Child Benefit

Child Benefit is a tax free benefit paid to people bringing up children. Your income is not taken into account – you can get Child Benefit however well off you are.

You can claim Child Benefit if you are bringing up a child who is under 16, or under 19 if the child is still in full-time education. If the child is not living with you, you must be paying the person looking after him or her at least as much as the Child Benefit. Normally the person the child is living with will claim Child Benefit.

Education benefits

Your children may be eligible for free transport to and from school, depending on how far you live from the school. Children will qualify for free school meals if you are on Income Support or Income-based Jobseeker's Allowance. They may be able to get an allowance for school clothes if your income is low. Grants for higher education are also available. Ask the department which provides educational services in your local authority for details.

National Health Service benefits

You may be able to get help with optical, dental and prescription charges if your income is low. Further details are available from the optician, dentist, doctor, chemist or Benefits Agency office.

Income tax

How splitting up affects your income tax

Cohabiting couples: While living together the income of each partner is assessed separately and liability for payment of tax remains with the individual concerned. Splitting up therefore has no effect on this aspect of your tax position. If you have children you can claim an additional personal allowance whether or not you are living with a partner; but you and your partner may claim only one allowance between you. On separation you and your partner can each claim an additional personal allowance so long as the claimant has at least one child living with her/him for the whole or part of the year.

Married couples: Since 1990/91 incomes of spouses have been subject to separate assessment so that while living together the position is similar to that of cohabiting couples. In addition a married couple is entitled to a married couple's allowance. The married couple's allowance can be claimed by either husband or wife or split equally between them.

You are treated as still living with your husband or wife unless:-

- you have been separated by a court order or by deed of separation; *or*

- you are separated in such circumstances that the separation is likely to be permanent.

When you first separate the partner who was claiming the married couple's allowance can continue to do so until the end of the tax year.

If you become reconciled in the tax year in which you separated you are treated as if you have never separated.

If married couples separate permanently, each partner should notify his/her tax office immediately. If you have children, either partner could be eligible for an additional personal allowance so long as the person claiming it has at least one child living with her/him for the whole or part of the year.

How maintenance is taxed

These rules apply to agreements or orders made after March 1988. Where a married couple is separated or divorced the husband (or wife) can claim tax relief up to a certain limit for maintenance paid through a court order, through a legally enforceable written agreement or through an assessment made by the Child Support Agency. Any maintenance paid above this figure is not eligible for tax relief. If the person receiving maintenance remarries the paying spouse will stop getting tax relief for the maintenance payments.

Voluntary maintenance payments do not qualify for tax relief and neither do maintenance payments made direct to a child. An unmarried parent cannot claim tax relief for any maintenance payments made whether they are to a child or a former partner.

Maintenance is not treated as income for tax purposes. A person in receipt of maintenance is not liable to pay tax on any maintenance received regardless of whether or not he or she is working or whether the order is payable to her/him or the children.

Tax relief on home loans

A couple who are married or live together can claim tax relief at the basic rate for the interest paid on the first £30,000 of their mortgage. (Unmarried partners who bought before 1.8.88. may be receiving tax relief on more than £30,000 but their combined tax relief will be restricted to £30,000 when they move, even if they transfer the existing mortgage.). On separation or divorce each partner can claim relief up to £30,000 for mortgages taken out to buy separate accommodation.

Who is going to pay the mortgage should be sorted out as soon as you can after separation in order to avoid arrears building up. The spouse who stays on in the home should take over the payments and if necessary be given additional aliment to enable that to be done. This gives the occupier relief on the existing loan and enables the absent spouse to obtain mortgage interest relief on accommodation he or she acquires.

If you take out or extend a mortgage in order to buy out your spouse's share of the home you can claim mortgage interest relief. Your tax inspector may ask for evidence that this is what the loan is for so it is a good idea for you and your spouse to put the arrangement in writing

Capital gains tax

Tax is not payable in respect of assets transferred between spouses while they are living together or in the tax year in which they separate. Assets transferred thereafter may result in tax being charged depending on the amount of the "gain" realised or the asset transferred. Your home is exempt.

CHAPTER SEVEN

ARRANGEMENTS FOR
THE CHILDREN

This chapter deals with the different arrangements that can be made for the children, and the legal position regarding where they should live, who can see them and guardianship.

Parental responsibilities and rights

Parental responsibilities agreement for parents who are not married
Deciding where the children should live
Step-children
How the court decides where the children should live
Can I see the children?
Enforcing your rights
How long does a residence order or contact order last?
Other orders the court can make

Guardianship

Court orders made before 1st November 1996

When you split up you and your partner will have to decide what is to happen to the children. Splitting up can be very difficult for children to cope with. Their home is broken up, they may have to leave their familiar surroundings and their friends, and they will be faced with the pressures of conflicting loyalties to each parent. Try to explain to the children about the splitting up and what is going to happen to them. They are probably more confused and upset than you realise and need to have someone to talk over their concerns with. By considering the children's needs you and your partner can help them to come through the process of splitting up relatively unscathed. Whatever else you disagree about, you should try to agree about the arrangements to be made for the children. Don't forget about the children's wishes – involve them in the discussions if they are old enough.

If the court has to get involved to solve problems it will ask your children for their views although they do not have to give them. It will take account of views of younger children according to age and maturity. It assumes that children of 12 or over are sufficiently mature to express a view. Various counselling agencies are available to help you and your partner reach a mutually acceptable solution - see Chapter 1 for further details.

Parental responsibilities and rights

During marriage each parent has equal parental responsibilities and rights for their children. When the parents are not married, the mother normally has full parental responsibilities and rights even when she lives with the father, unless they have made a parental responsibility agreement (see below) or he has a court order giving him parental responsibilities and rights. Parental responsibilities are to :-

- safeguard and promote a child's health, development and welfare until the child is 16; *and*

- provide direction until a child is 16 and guidance until 18; *and*

- maintain direct and regular contact until a child is 16; *and*

- act on behalf of a child in legal transactions until s/he is 16.

Parental rights are what the law says parents have to allow them to meet their responsibilities. These rights are:-

- to have the child live with you or to say where the child is to live. (You cannot take the child out of the country without the permission of any other person with parental responsibilities and rights. This would break civil law. However if there is an existing UK court order about who is to look after the child or against removing the child from the UK, a person who takes the child out of the country without the permission of the carer or the court will be breaking criminal law.); *and*

- to organise, control and change if necessary, how the child is brought up; *and*

- to have a relationship with the child and to see him/her regularly; *and*

- to act on behalf of the child in legal transactions until s/he is 16.

When parents are splitting up, they can agree to continue to share these responsibilities and rights.

Parental responsibilities agreement for parents who are not married

It is possible for an unmarried couple to agree that they want to share parental responsibilities and rights. This can be done relatively easily by obtaining a form called a Parental Responsibilities and Parental Rights Agreement from a local Registrar's office. This is where people have to go to register a birth or a death. Both parents must sign the form and it must be witnessed. When there is more than one child the parents must fill in a form for each child. Once it has been signed and witnessed it must be sent to the Registers of Scotland (see p30 for address) who will register it in a public register the Books of Council and Session. The agreement means that the parents have equal parental responsibilities and rights. Once it has been made, if a mother wanted to go back to having sole parental rights and responsibilities, she would have to go to court.

Deciding where the children should live

One of the most difficult decisions that parents who are splitting up will have to take is who the children should live with. When the parents can agree, it may be possible to make arrangements between them quite privately. However, if the parent who cares for the children most of the time needed financial assistance in the form of benefits or child support, the couple would need to inform the Child Support Agency what the arrangements were.

When parents are divorcing they can agree about where the children should live but they must tell the court what arrangements have been made for the children. As long as the court is satisfied that the arrangements suit the children and the parents, it is unlikely to make any orders for the children. If the arrangements later break down either parent can apply to court to ask it to decide where the children should live.

When parents cannot agree and the court is asked to decide where a child should live, it can make an order called a "residence order". This may state that a child is to live with only one of the parents but it could state that the child is to spend some time with one parent and some time with another. In certain circumstances it can state that a child is to stay regularly with other members of the family, for example, a grandmother, as well as the periods with each parent.

When the court makes a residence order it states where the child is to live. It does not change any of the other parental responsibilities and rights each parent has. These could only be changed by other specific court orders. In practice it may mean that a parent who has the children living with him/her most of the time has to take most of the day to day decisions about the care of the child. However, the other parent will be able to challenge any decisions that are taken. If one parent does not want the other one to have any parental responsibilities or rights for the children, for example, because there has been abuse or violence, an application would have to be made to the court for a removal of the other parent's responsibilities and rights.

When there is a dispute about where the child should live and a person who does not have parental responsibilities and rights, for example, an unmarried father, wants to look after the child s/he can ask the court to grant a residence order. If the court agrees, the granting of the residence order also gives that person full parental responsibilities and rights. An unmarried father would then share these with the mother unless a court had removed them from her.

When a court is asked to decide about where a child should live it may also make an order stating who can see the child. This is called a "contact" order see p91.

Step-children

On separation you do not have any rights to have your stepchildren (your husband's or wife's children by a former marriage) living with you, simply because you are married to their parent. If you want them to live with you for even part of the time and their father or mother does not agree you will have to apply to court. You may wish to see them but are being told that you cannot. In this case you would have to apply to court for a "contact" order see p91.

Where you and your husband or wife have jointly adopted his or her children (your stepchildren) you will have equal parental responsibilities and rights automatically. From April 1997 a step-parent can apply to adopt alone and this gives rise to the same result.

How the court decides where the children should live

You can apply to the court for a residence order either as part of the divorce proceedings or in independent proceedings. If you are not married you have to use independent proceedings if you need the court to take decisions about the children. If you want to make sure that the children can live with you as soon as you and your partner separate, perhaps to prevent your partner interfering with or removing the children or to strengthen your position in case disputes arise later, you would be best to go for a court order independently of any divorce action. You may need to have a court order showing that the children live with you in order to obtain accommodation for yourself and the children. Some local authorities may insist on a court order before accepting you onto their housing waiting list or providing you with accommodation.

Many married couples, however, are content to leave formal regulation of where the children should live until a divorce action is brought. As soon as such an action is started an application can be made for *Interim* orders. These would last until the divorce action is heard, at which time the court will consider the question of where the children should live again. However, the court will not want to make an order for residence if you and your spouse seem to be working it out between yourselves.

If there is a dispute between you and your partner, the court decides on the basis of what is best for the children. Their welfare is the court's paramount consideration but the court will only make an order if it is necessary to make sure that the child's welfare is maintained.

A special court hearing called a "Child Welfare Hearing" will be called to try and resolve any disputes regarding a child. If the dispute is resolved, the court may make an order at this hearing but can also decide to leave the matter of court orders to a later hearing. All parties to the dispute, usually the parents, must attend the hearing. The child will only be asked to go if s/he has said that s/he wants to make her/his views known. The hearing will usually be held in private and may be quite informal. However, you may find it helpful to discuss what to expect at the hearing with your solicitor.

If the dispute cannot be resolved at the Child Welfare Hearing the case will have to be considered further by the court.

The factors it takes into account include:

- What sort of home each of you could offer; *and*

- How much personal attention each of you would give the children; *and*

- The conduct and character of you and your partner and any new partner either of you has; *and*

- The likely stability of any new relationship which you or your partner have formed; *and*

- Whether the children should be moved; *and*

- The views of the children.

To help it decide who the children are to live with the court may appoint a person usually an advocate or a social worker, to prepare an independent report on the situation. This person will interview you and your partner, any new partner either of you has, and look at the accommodation that would be provided for the children in each case. He or she may also interview neighbours, relatives, teachers at school and doctors.

The court is unwilling to disturb the children unnecessarily. So if the children have been living with you since the separation, but you and your partner are now in dispute about how many days of the week each of you should have them, or you only want your partner to have contact with the children but not let them stay over-night, the court will use any information it has about how the existing arrangements have been going to inform its decision.

The views of children as to which parent they would prefer to live with and see are very important. Your children will be sent a form called Form F asking them if they want to let the court know what they think. They may even ask a solicitor to represent them. They do not have to say anything but the court has to make sure that they have had the chance to say what they think. It assumes that a child of 12 or over has the maturity to express a view, but will take account of views of younger children according to their age and maturity.

Can I see the children?

When you and your partner split up your rights to see the children depend on the parental responsibilities that you have. As long as these have not been taken away from you, you have a right to see them. This may be sorted out by

- informal arrangements made with your partner; *or*

- what the court has ordered.

You and your partner should think about and discuss what sort of arrangements for contact would be best for you and the children.

Remember to involve the children in your discussions if they are old enough. Counselling and mediation services (see Chapter 1) are available to help find an arrangement acceptable to all of you. The arrangement need not be rigid - for example you could be allowed to come and see the children whenever it was convenient.

As a means of keeping in contact, having the children to stay with you over a weekend or during part of the holidays may be better than visiting them in your partner's home or taking them out for a few hours. An outing every Sunday afternoon can turn into a chore for you and the children instead of being something to look forward to. Different ages of children need different types of arrangement. An older child will appreciate some individual contact with you rather than always seeing you with younger brothers or sisters.

Contact may well be upsetting for both of you and the children just after the split up. Maintaining contact with both parents during this difficult period is important for the children, because once contact is lost it is not easy to re-establish. If you cannot see the children you may be able to keep in touch in other ways, such as telephoning, letters or occasional presents. Getting information about their progress from the school will also help you to feel involved.

It is unwise for you to set the children against their other parent. If he or she has been awarded contact you have a duty to encourage the children to see or go with him or her unless you are convinced that this would be bad for them. If you are the parent who has a court order for contact you should not question the children too closely about their home life as the other might resent it as prying.

If the court has made a residence order stating that the children are to live most of the time with one parent it is likely to make a contact order for the other partner unless there is evidence that seeing the other partner is not in the children's interests. The court will as a general rule consider that it is in a child's best interests to grow up knowing and having contact with both parents and any other significant people in their lives, for example, grandparents.

When contact has not been regulated by the court you are entitled to reasonable contact with the children. However, if you disrupt the children's life too much by demanding to see them at unreasonable hours, your partner may decide to apply to the court for regulation of contact.

Where you and your partner cannot agree about contact, either of you can apply to the court for an order regulating it. The court will decide on the basis of the welfare of the children. Contact will not be imposed on children against their wishes. Contact would also be refused to a parent leading a dissolute life or likely to hurt the children. One situation that creates difficulties is where a woman who separated because of her partner's violence is afraid to allow him contact because he might trace her through the children. Practice varies as to whether contact will be refused on this ground.

When a contact order is made by the court it states how and when contact is to take place - for example, visiting every Sunday afternoon between 2 and 6 or having the children to stay for a week every school holiday. The court can order supervised contact only in the presence of another person if it is concerned for the children's safety or possible non-return.

Enforcing your rights

If you have a residence order you are entitled to have the children living with you for the times stated on the order unless a court or a children's hearing has ordered that they should live elsewhere, because, for example, they need extra supervision or protection..

If you have a contact order you are entitled to see the children at the times stated on the order.

If another person refuses to hand the children over to you, you will have to go to court for an order requiring the person to deliver them to you. Failure to obey such a delivery order is a contempt of court and the person can be fined or imprisoned. The court may also authorise a sheriff officer to search for the children and hand them over to you.

See p22 for what to do if you fear that the children will be taken out of the United Kingdom against your wishes or "snatched" from you.

How long does a residence order or contact order last?

A court order for residence or contact is not final; it can be changed later if the circumstances change. For example, if you have acquired a suitable home, or remarried, or now have a job which doesn't mean you have to go abroad frequently, you could apply to the court for the children to stay with you more often and for both of you to have a residence order. The court is, however, normally reluctant to shunt children around. Before ordering a change of arrangements for the care of the children it would have to be satisfied that your new situation is likely to be permanent, and that there would be long term advantages to the children in the changes.

Residence and contact orders end when the child reaches the age of 16 because this is the age at which a parent stops having the right to have the child live with him/her or the right to maintain contact. However, a parent has the responsibility to guide a child until s/he is 18 but cannot be forced to do so, nor does the child have to follow the guidance.

Other orders the court can make

There may be a range of issues about the children over which you and your partner cannot agree. As long as you both have parental responsibilities and rights (see p87) you each have the right to take decisions about for example, where a child should go to school, what medical treatment s/he requires or any other major aspects of the child's upbringing. Each parent can exercise parental responsibilities and rights and a third party can take action on a decision by one parent alone. If one parent has not been consulted by the other and wishes to stop what the other parent is doing or the decision that has been taken, the court can be asked to decide on the issue, either as part of divorce proceedings, or on its own. The court may also be asked to decide on the issue if a third party is insisting on having the consent of both parents. The order the court makes is called a "specific issue order".

Guardianship

A guardian has full parental responsibilities and rights .

A guardian can be appointed in a will and if only one parent has died will be expected to take on the role of parent along with the surviving parent. You should ask a potential guardian before you appoint him/her in a will to check that there is a willingness to do it. You may also wish to discuss the issue with a child who is old enough to understand and take the child's views into account in selecting someone to take on the role.

A court may appoint a guardian for a child either if the child's parents die and there is no guardian appointed in a will, or if the parents or other people who have parental responsibilities and rights for the child are unsuitable to look after the child and have these responsibilities taken away by the court.

When you split up from a partner who has no parental responsibilities or rights or has had them taken away by a court it may be useful for your peace of mind to appoint a guardian to make sure that the children will be looked after by someone you want to care for them in the event of your death.

Court orders made before 1st November 1996

You may have a court order from a divorce or separation that was made before 1st November 1996. These court orders are still legal. You may have:-

- a custody order - you have total rights for the day to day care of the children but your partner may have a number of rights granted by the court;

- an access order - you have the right to see the children, probably at a specified time.

If you or your partner go back to court to have the orders for custody or access reviewed by the court, the issues will be considered under the new arrangements for "residence" and "contact" as described in this chapter.

CHAPTER EIGHT

GETTING
DIVORCED

This chapter looks at the legal proceedings involved in getting divorced.

Can I get divorced in Scotland?

Which court?
Grounds for divorce
Adultery
Behaviour
Desertion
Non-cohabitation

DIY divorce

Ordinary divorce procedure

Starting the action
Interim orders
Contested actions
Reconciliation
Affidavit evidence
Care of the children
Granting the divorce
Notification of divorce

What will it cost?

DIY divorces
Ordinary divorce procedure
Legal aid charge

Can I get divorced in Scotland?

You can get divorced in Scotland if:-

- you or your husband or wife are domiciled in Scotland – meaning Scotland is regarded as the permanent home – at the date of bringing the action; *or*

- you or your husband or wife have been habitually resident in Scotland for at least a year before bringing the action.

The rules for bringing actions in England or Wales are very similar. So if you are domiciled in Scotland and your husband or wife is domiciled in England or Wales you have a choice. You can bring your divorce action either in Scotland or in England or Wales.

Which court?

Your divorce action will be heard either by the Court of Session - situated in Edinburgh - or your local sheriff court. You can choose but you will not usually get legal aid for a Court of Session divorce. The appropriate sheriff court for your divorce action is the one serving the area where you or your husband or wife have been living for at least 40 days before bringing the action. If you and your husband or wife have separated and live in different sheriff court areas, then you will have a choice of sheriff court.

Grounds for divorce

The court will grant you a divorce if you can show that your marriage has irretrievably broken down because of:

- your husband's or wife's adultery; *or*

- your husband or wife has behaved in such a way that you cannot reasonably be expected to live with him or her; *or*

- your husband or wife has deserted you *and* has not lived with you for 2 years; *or*

- you have not lived with your husband or wife for a least 2 years *and* he or she agrees to the divorce; *or*

- you have not lived with your husband or wife for at least 5 years.

You do not have to wait for 2 years before you can get a divorce on either of the first two grounds.

Adultery

Your husband or wife commits adultery if he or she has sexual intercourse voluntarily with a person of the opposite sex other than you at any time during the marriage. Adultery committed after you and your husband or wife split up for some other reason is also a valid ground for divorce.

You cannot get a divorce based on any act of adultery if you condoned it. This means that you knew about it and forgave your husband or wife. If you continue or resume living together as any normal couple would for more than a 3 month period after discovering the adultery, it is assumed that you have forgiven it. But living separate lives in the same house because neither of you can find alternative accommodation does not count as forgiving.

You cannot get a divorce if you actively encourage your wife's or husband's adultery. Thus, for example, if you both take part in sex parties or similar activities, neither of you can get a divorce on the basis of your partner's adultery.

Continuing adultery is usually proved by means of private detectives who visit your husband or wife and his or her new partner. Past adultery is more difficult to prove; indirect evidence such as having shared a bedroom is acceptable.

Behaviour

You can divorce your husband or wife for behaving in such a way that you cannot reasonably be expected to live with him or her. This behaviour must have occurred after the date of your marriage. All kinds of behaviour can lead to a divorce whether it affects you, the children or others, such as relations. The test is whether you, as the kind of person you are, can reasonably be expected to live with your husband or wife. So the court will take into account the standard of conduct you expect from your partner in judging his or her behaviour. Unreasonable behaviour normally consists of positive acts such as assaults, threats of violence, insulting or domineering conduct or regular drunkenness. But it can also be omissions such as indifference to your husband or wife, unreasonable refusal of sexual relations, or spending so much time on your hobbies or sports that your husband or wife is excluded from your life. It may be a single act or continuing conduct. Unreasonable sexual demands or sexual acts with another person short of adultery (such as homosexual acts) may also form grounds for divorce.

You cannot complain of your husband's or wife's unreasonable behaviour if it is due to a disease, old age or an accident. For example a man who is fit and well yet spends all day in bed could find himself divorced, but a man who becomes bedridden due to a car crash could not be divorced. However, you can get a divorce if your husband's or wife's behaviour is due to insanity or mental abnormality.

If you are intending to sue for divorce on grounds of behaviour, you should tell people such as neighbours or relations of the incidents as they occur, so that they will be in a position to give evidence if required. Also if you become physically or mentally ill as a result of your husband's or wife's behaviour, you should see your doctor and state the cause of your illness, rather than cover up. Your doctor will then be in a position to certify, if required, that your husband's or wife's conduct has adversely affected your health. The police may be able to provide evidence if they were called after your husband or wife had assaulted you.

Desertion

Your husband or wife deserts you if:-

- he or she voluntarily lives apart from you but you wish to live together; *and*

- for a period of two years after he or she left you have continued to live apart; *and*

- you have not refused a genuine and reasonable offer to live together again.

Your husband or wife must mean to leave you. If he or she is sent to prison or goes into hospital, that is not desertion. Taking up employment abroad against your wishes would be desertion if it would be unreasonable for you to accompany him or her. You cannot get a divorce for desertion if you have given your husband or wife reasonable cause for leaving you, such as your adultery or unreasonable behaviour. The partner who deserts is usually the one who leaves the home but this is not always the case. For example, if your husband beats you and throws you out of the home, it is he who is in desertion, not you. Or if he gets a better job in another place and you refuse to join him there, you will be treated as deserting him. If you want to use desertion as a ground for divorce you must have lived apart from your husband or wife for a total period of 2 years.

But this period does not have to be unbroken, as long as the periods when you live together do not exceed 6 months. If they do a fresh 2 year period during which you live apart has to elapse.

Example: Andrew deserted Jean on 1 January 1993. They were reconciled and lived together from 1 January to 30 April 1994 and then split up finally. Jean can start a divorce action on 1 May 1995. But if the reconciliation lasted until 31 July 1994, no action can be taken until 1 August 1996.

Non-cohabitation

You can get a divorce if you have not lived together with your husband or wife for a certain period. This period is 2 years if your husband or wife agrees to you bringing divorce proceedings, otherwise it is 5 years.

The reason why you are not living together does not matter. As long as your husband or wife is away - in hospital, in prison or working abroad for example - for the requisite period you can get a divorce.

Living together means living as a married couple normally would. If you and your husband or wife stop sleeping together and lead separate lives in the same house, you are not living together as a normal couple.

If you and your husband or wife resume living together again for a period or periods totalling more than 6 months after the initial separation and then separate finally, you must wait for another 2 or 5 years before divorce is possible. As long as you do not live together for more than 6 months in all a fresh period is unnecessary, although you cannot count the time you have spent living together towards the 2 or 5 year period. See the example above which shows how similar rules work for the 2 year desertion period.

The court may not grant a divorce on the basis of 5 years non-cohabitation if your husband or wife would suffer grave financial hardship because of the divorce. In practice grave financial hardship is never invoked as the court has power to share matrimonial property including future pension rights (see p64).

If you are divorcing your husband or wife on the basis of 2 years non-cohabitation he or she must consent to the divorce being granted. Your husband or wife is entitled to give consent on conditions, for example that you do not ask for any financial award, or that the children live with him or her. The court will not interfere with these conditions. If you find them unacceptable you will have to wait a further 3 years so that you can get a divorce on the ground of 5 years non-cohabitation, or find some other ground, such as adultery.

Your husband or wife can withdraw his or her consent at any time before the court grants a divorce.

DIY divorce

You can get a divorce without a solicitor by using the DIY procedure (properly called the simplified procedure). You can use this procedure if the grounds of divorce are non-cohabitation for 2 or 5 years. In the case of the 2 year period your husband or wife must consent to the divorce.

Certain conditions must also apply:

- The divorce is uncontested; *and*

- There are no children of the marriage under 16 years old; *and*

- No financial claims are being made; *and*

- There are no other proceedings affecting your marriage which have still to be heard; *and*

- Neither you nor your husband or wife is suffering from mental disorder.

You can obtain the necessary forms from your local sheriff court, the Court of Session or a Citizens Advice Bureau. You will also get an easy-to-understand leaflet which tells you how to complete the forms. The basic cost is £55, but if you are on Income Support or Income-based Job Seekers Allowance or have a low income or are seeing a solicitor under the Legal Advice and Assistance Scheme, this fee is waived. You will have to obtain a copy of your marriage certificate if you have not already got one.

Once you have completed the forms you send them to the court (the Court of Session or your local sheriff court) which then sends a copy to your husband or wife by post. If the copy cannot be delivered by post, you will have to pay for the copy to be served in another way. You can expect to obtain a divorce within 2 months of lodging the forms in court.

Ordinary divorce procedure

If you think you have grounds for divorce but you cannot use the DIY procedure, go and see a solicitor. He or she will discuss whether you have grounds, what financial orders you might apply for and whether you should apply for court orders for where the children should live and who should have contact with them.

Starting the action

If your solicitor is satisfied that you have grounds for divorce he or she will then lodge with the court a document which sets out your claims and the evidence and arguments in support of them. This document has to be served on your husband or wife, usually by post. If you are seeking a divorce on the grounds of adultery, a copy must also be served on the person with whom you allege your husband or wife committed adultery.

In the cases of non-cohabitation for 2 or 5 years a notice is sent to your husband or wife with the document. This notice warns of the consequences of divorce on their inheritance and pension rights and contains information about the financial orders they can apply for.

If you are asking for orders in relation to the children, a summary in simple language has to be sent to the children if they are old enough to understand (8 or over is usual).

Interim orders

Once divorce proceedings have started you can ask for various interim orders. They are called interim orders because they only last until the divorce action is heard, although some of them may be renewed then.

These interim orders include:-

- interim aliment for you (see p23);

- interim residence order for the children (see p21) and/or an interdict against their removal from your control or out of Scotland;

- an interim interdict prohibiting your husband or wife from assaulting or molesting you (see p16);

- an interim exclusion order (see p17);

- an order preventing your husband or wife disposing of his or her property in order to defeat your claim for financial provision.

Your husband or wife will normally be given an opportunity to object to your application so you should have your evidence ready to support it.

Contested actions

Your husband or wife can contest your action of divorce, although the vast majority are uncontested. More commonly your husband or wife will object to your claims for financial orders or court orders for the care of the children, or apply for these themselves. If there are any matters related to the children in dispute, the court will hold a Child Welfare Hearing. (see p90)

If your husband or wife contests the case, a preliminary hearing has to take place in sheriff court cases. This is called an Options Hearing. You, your husband or wife and your respective solicitors attend. The sheriff will find out what the issues are, what can be agreed and what remains to be decided by witnesses giving evidence in court. But if only your claims for court orders for the care of the children or financial orders are objected to, you can still use affidavit evidence (see below) for the divorce.

Reconciliation

If you and your husband or wife attempt a reconciliation once the divorce proceedings are under way the court can, if asked, stop proceedings to see how it works out. If the reconciliation does not work, the fact that you and your husband lived together will not prevent you obtaining a divorce.

Affidavit evidence

Instead of having to give evidence orally in court, you and your witnesses may be able to give evidence by means of a sworn statement called an affidavit. It is not a good idea to rely on affidavit evidence for important aspects of your case if it is contested. Such evidence is regarded as less reliable than oral evidence in court. Your solicitor will prepare the affidavit for you and the witnesses to sign, and you should make sure that the statements contained in it reflect the up-to-date position, otherwise a further affidavit will be necessary. A second affidavit would be required if the position changes after the first affidavit is lodged in court, or the court requires additional information.

Care of the children

Before the court grants a divorce it must be satisfied that the arrangements being made for any children are satisfactory or the best that can be devised in the circumstances.

Where you and your husband or wife agree as to where the children are to live, the court usually accepts the agreed arrangements. A person who knows the children well – a grandparent or a neighbour for example – will have to give affidavit evidence of the children's circumstances and of the suitability of the proposed arrangements.

If you and your husband or wife cannot agree on future arrangements for the children, the court will hold a Child Welfare Hearing. You and your husband or wife must attend and the children may attend or give their views some other way. The court attempts to resolve matters at the Hearing. If agreement cannot be reached the court will require much more information to enable it to settle the dispute (see Chapter 7).

Granting the divorce

Where the court is satisfied that you are entitled to a divorce and that the care of the children is settled it will grant a divorce. It is possible to leave the financial matters outstanding to a later date, although it is normally better to have everything dealt with at the same time.

Notification of divorce

You or your solicitor will be told when the court grants the divorce. Your husband or wife has 14 days in which to appeal in the case of a sheriff court divorce (21 days in the Court of Session). After that, if no appeal is taken, you can obtain from the court a document showing the divorce and any orders which the court made on finance, care of the children and other matters.

The court will inform your husband or wife of the divorce if their address is known. If you were married in Scotland the Registrar General for Scotland is also informed so that the divorce can be registered.

What will it cost?

The expenses of any legal proceedings consist of your solicitor's fees, and outlays such as postage, telephone calls and money paid by your solicitor to others involved in the case (such as an advocate or sheriff officer). Even in an ordinary undefended divorce these can amount to £700, while the expenses of a defended divorce can easily exceed £5,000.

DIY divorces

You can recover your expenses from your husband or wife only if he or she agreed to pay them.

Ordinary divorce procedure

The court has a complete discretion in deciding whether one person should pay their opponent's expenses as well as their own. Certain rules set out below are, however, usually followed. If the proceedings result in an agreed settlement that should also deal with liability for expenses.

When there is no agreement as to expenses the court will deal with them at the end of the proceedings. Two important factors are who won and whether the proceedings were conducted in a reasonable way. Making exaggerated claims, refusing a reasonable offer or attempting to hide assets may result in you having to pay most or all of your spouse's expenses as well as your own. Most divorces result in partial success for each spouse and often each is left to pay his or her own expenses. Consent may be given to a divorce on the grounds of non-cohabitation for two years on condition that the consenter is not liable for the other's expenses. This condition is quite common and will be enforced.

Where one spouse is on legal aid the courts do not generally award expenses against him or her. The non-legally aided spouse will almost always have to pay his or her own expenses and might well have to pay the other's as well.

The legal aid charge

If you are legally aided and the Scottish Legal Aid Board fails to recover the amount it has spent on your action from your contributions (if any) and the expenses your husband or wife has been ordered to pay by the court, the Board can recover the balance out of any sums awarded to you or property which you recover or is preserved for you as a result of your action.

This rule does not apply to court orders for aliment or periodical allowance. It *does apply* to awards of lump sums or transfers of property on divorce over £2,500 and other orders in different proceedings.

You should take the charge into account before embarking on litigation. Even if you are successful you may end up with little or nothing. See p114 for further details.

CHAPTER NINE

JUDICIAL SEPARATION
AND NULLITY

This chapter looks at judicial separation and nullity actions.

Getting a judicial separation

Should I get divorced or separated?

Getting your marriage annulled

Getting a judicial separation

You can apply to the court for a judicial separation instead of a divorce. The grounds are exactly the same (see p97). Judicial separations are rather uncommon nowadays.

Should I get divorced or separated?

The advantages of judicial separation over divorce are:-

- you remain entitled to widow's benefits or a pension from the state or your husband's pension scheme, should your husband die before you;

- you may object to divorce on religious grounds;

- your occupancy rights in the home do not come to an end.

The disadvantages are:-

- you are still married so that you cannot remarry;

- you cannot ask the court for a capital sum or a transfer of property (you can only get aliment). However, you and your husband or wife can come to a separate agreement about these.

A decree of separation does not prohibit your partner from living with you or visiting you. If you want to stop your partner doing this, you must get an exclusion order (see p17).

Any property a wife acquires after getting a judicial separation from her husband will not go to him if she dies without leaving a will. There is no equivalent rule for a husband's property.

Because the grounds for separation and divorce are the same, once you have got a decree of separation you can get a divorce later (if you want to remarry for example) without having to re-prove the facts you proved in your separation action.

Getting your marriage annulled

Your marriage can be annulled because it was not valid or because of sexual impotency.

A Scottish marriage is not valid if:-

- you and your partner were under 16 at the date of the ceremony; *or*

- you or your partner were already married to someone else at the date of the ceremony; *or*

- you or your partner were insane at the date of the ceremony or did not consent to get married; *or*

- you and your partner are too closely related to each other; *or*

- you and your partner are of the same sex; *or*

- you or you partner were domiciled abroad (i.e. had your permanent home abroad) at the date of the marriage and the law there did not permit you to marry.

Your marriage can be annulled if either you or your partner was impotent – incapable of normal sexual intercourse – at the time of the marriage and has remained impotent thereafter. You cannot have your marriage annulled if your partner becomes impotent after the marriage. The incapacity may be due to a physical defect or psychological causes. It must be incurable, or the affected person must refuse to be treated. Psychological impotence arising after marriage may give you grounds for divorce on the basis of your partner's behaviour (see p98).

The court has the same powers to make financial awards in nullity actions as it has in divorce actions (see p63).

Nullity actions are rare. You should consult a solicitor if you think you have grounds for having your marriage annulled.

CHAPTER TEN

EFFECTS OF DIVORCE
OR SEPARATION

This chapter looks at some effects of divorce or separation.

Nationality and immigration

Cohabitees

Welfare benefits

Changing names

Nationality and immigration

If you were a British citizen, a Commonwealth citizen with right of abode in the UK or a "settled" person before your marriage, splitting up will not affect your right to enter and live in the UK. Rights you acquired because of your marriage may be affected. How they may be affected is set out below.

If you marry a British citizen, a Commonwealth citizen with right of abode or a settled person you will be given permission initially to stay in the UK for 12 months. You will not be given permission to stay as a husband or wife if you are under 16, but you may qualify for entry in your own right. At the end of 12 months you may apply to the Home Office for settled status. If you have separated or divorced before you apply your application will almost certainly be refused unless there are exceptional compassionate circumstances.

Once you have been given settled status, separation or divorce should not affect your right to stay in the UK. A settled person can apply for British citizenship after having lived in the UK for a certain period. This period is 3 years if you are still married at the date of application, otherwise it is 5 years. Once you are a British citizen your status is not affected by a subsequent separation or divorce.

If you married an EU worker (a citizen of one of the member countries of the European Union working or looking for work in the UK) you will be allowed to stay in the UK for as long as he or she does. Separation should not affect this right but divorce will probably mean that you are expected to leave the UK. The Home Office should only take action if they have strong grounds for believing that it was only a marriage of convenience.

If you are married to a person who has been given permission to stay in the UK for a limited time (for instance as a student or a work permit holder) separation or divorce will mean you have to qualify in your own right if you want to stay.

Cohabitees

Cohabitees may be entitled to come to or stay in the U.K. in their own right. If so, splitting up will not affect their right to stay. If not, there is a concession arrangement outwith the normal immigration rules for partners of many classes of people, including British citizens and those with settled status. The relationship must be akin to marriage, have lasted for at least four years, any previous marriage or relationship must have broken down permanently and the couple must intend to live together permanently (or at least while they are in the U.K.). You should seek further information if you need to rely on the concessionary arrangement to enter or stay in the U.K.

Welfare benefits

After divorce you will not be entitled to any widow's benefits based on your ex-husband's contributions should he die subsequently. See p74 for how divorce affects your rights under your ex-husband's or ex-wife's private pension scheme.

If you divorce before you reach retirement age your state retirement pension is calculated on either your own contribution record, or your ex-husband's or ex-wife's record whether or not they re-married if that will give you a higher pension. Retirement age is currently 65 for a man and 60 for a woman though the pension age for women born after March 1955 may be raised to 65. You can only rely on your ex-husband's or ex-wife's record as long as neither of you remarry. On your remarriage before retirement age, your future pension will be calculated on the basis of your own contributions, or those of your new husband or wife, whichever gives you a better pension.

If you divorce after retirement age, you should inform your local Benefits Agency office at once, so that your and your ex-husband's or ex-wife's pensions can be adjusted.

Separation has no effect on your entitlement to widow's benefits or a retirement pension. But you will lose your widow's benefits if you are living with another man.

Changing names

On splitting up a woman may wish to change back to her own name, but she is entitled to continue using her (ex)husband's name if she wants to.

A mother may want to change her children's surnames to that of her new husband when she remarries. You should think carefully before you do this. It may make things easier for you, your husband and the children to have the same surname in that your divorce is concealed. On the other hand, the children's father (and perhaps the children too) may resent a change. Nowadays, with so many marriages breaking up, it has ceased to be embarrassing for children to have different names from the adults looking after them.

You can change your and the children's names simply by telling everyone concerned (employer, doctor, school, etc) of the new name. Personal documents such as child benefit books and passports will have to be altered. A change in the children's names can be registered in an official register, the Register of Corrections Etc, if the children were born in Scotland. The advantage of official registration is that a new birth certificate can be obtained showing their new names. To register a change you should see your local Registrar of Births, Deaths and Marriages. If the children's father was married to you, he must agree to any change and sign the appropriate forms

Appendix one

Legal aid

Free initial interview

Many solicitors are prepared to give a free initial interview of up to half an hour. In this way you can get preliminary advice on your difficulties, at no cost even if you would not qualify for legal advice and assistance or legal aid. When you first contact a solicitor ask if this service is available.

You can be helped to pay for legal services if you cannot afford to pay a solicitor yourself. There are two different schemes: legal advice and assistance, and legal aid. Most solicitors undertake legal aid work. A list of those who do can be obtained from the Law Society of Scotland, 26 Drumsheugh Gardens, Edinburgh EH3 7YR (tel.: 0131-226 7411) or your local Citizens Advice Bureau or Sheriff Court.

The amounts of money mentioned below change fairly frequently. They were correct as at the date of writing this book, but will give a rough guide only as to the position in the future.

Children aged 12 or over can apply for legal advice and assistance or legal aid. Younger children may apply if they are capable of understanding what asking a solicitor to act involves. Parents may apply on behalf of a child up to age 16.

Legal advice and assistance

Under this scheme (sometimes called the pink form scheme) you can receive up to £80 worth of legal help, although more may be authorised if an application is made by your solicitor for an increase. Almost any kind of help on matters the Scottish courts can deal with may be provided, such as advising on your rights to aliment, occupancy of the house or an inheritance. A solicitor can also prepare a separation agreement under the scheme. Court or tribunal appearances are not covered although your solicitor can help you to present your case yourself. Legal advice and assistance is also useful for getting preliminary advice and paying for initial investigations to see whether you have a good case for which legal aid could be obtained to begin court proceedings. In this case and if you are likely to qualify for legal aid the initial limit is increased to £150.

Legal advice and assistance is free if your savings (excluding your home and contents) are less than £1000 and your net income (after tax, and national insurance contributions) is below £72 per week. Advice and assistance is free to an applicant who is in receipt of (or whose partner is in receipt of) Income Support, Income-based Jobseeker's Allowance or Family Credit. The figure for savings is much larger if you are of pensionable age. If your net income is more than £172 per week you will not get any help under the scheme. In between £72 and £172 you have to pay a proportion of the cost according to a sliding scale. All these figures are increased if you have dependants living with you.

Your spouse's or cohabiting partner's savings and income is added to yours in order to see whether you qualify for legal advice and assistance. But this rule does not apply if you are claiming against your husband, wife or partner or defending a claim made by him or her, or if you are living apart.

Legal aid

Under this scheme you can get help with the expenses of legal proceedings before the courts. Examples where legal aid may be available include proceedings for divorce, aliment, occupancy rights or an interdict against violence. The scheme does not cover matters such as house purchase or advice relating to tax or benefits since you are not making or defending a claim.

In order to get legal aid:

- the Scottish Legal Aid Board must be satisfied that you have a reasonable case, and that it is reasonable that you should be legally aided. Your solicitor may need to do some work beforehand investigating and getting evidence for your claim. You can get help with the cost of the preliminary work by means of the legal advice and assistance scheme, as legal aid generally only helps with expenses incurred after you have been granted legal aid. *and*

- your disposable income must be below £8,571 per year (after tax, housing costs and allowances for dependants living with you). Legal Aid is free if your disposable income is below £2,625. Between £2,625 and £8,571 a contribution is required, paid over ten monthly instalments. If your capital is below £3,000 no contribution will be required from capital. Between £3,000 and £8,560 a lump sum will be required and over £8,560 legal aid is not available. Your spouse or cohabiting partner's income and savings will be counted in, unless you are claiming against your husband, wife or partner, or defending a claim by him or her, or if you are living apart. Your house and contents are not counted as savings but life policies and business interests are included.

If you are successful in your claim your opponent normally has to pay your expenses, but see p105 for the rules on divorce expenses. Where the Scottish Legal Aid Board recovers these expenses in full from your opponent, you will have any contributions you paid towards your legal aid refunded. A refund may, however, take a long time to be paid. If you lose your case the normal rule is that you have to pay your opponent's expenses as well as your own, but see p105 for the rules on divorce expenses. The court will not normally order you to pay your opponent's expenses if you are legally aided. If you are ordered to pay and your opponent is legally aided, the Scottish Legal Aid Board will ask you for further contributions, over and above those you have already paid. If your opponent is not legally aided and you are ordered to pay his or her expenses, then his or her solicitor will ask you for payment.

Specially urgent work can be done before applying for legal aid but an application must be made within 28 days. Your solicitor must be satisfied that the work is urgently necessary and that you are likely to qualify for legal aid.

The legal aid charge

If you are legally aided the Scottish Legal Aid Board recovers the amount it has spent on your legal proceedings from your contributions (if any) and any expenses your opponent has been ordered to pay by the court. Any amount still due will be recovered out of the money or property awarded to or preserved for you. This amount is called the Legal Aid Charge. It applies also to money or property made over to or preserved for you under an agreement you and your partner made to avoid going to court or to settle legal proceedings.

The Legal Aid Charge does not apply to:-

- any aliment; *or*

- any periodical allowance awarded on divorce or nullity; *or*

- the first £2,500 of any capital sum awarded or property transferred to you on divorce or nullity.

These exceptions apply to court orders and agreements made to avoid or settle legal proceedings.

Legal proceedings beyond an undefended divorce action can be very expensive. The Charge may well swallow up most of your award. You and your partner should avoid contested proceedings and appeals if at all possible.

Where you have been awarded (a share of) the home or a lump sum to enable you to buy yourself a new home the Board may postpone the Charge instead of requiring you to sell the house or to give up part of your lump sum to pay it. If the Charge is postponed the Board will take a security over your home. This means that when you eventually sell your home you will have to pay the Charge plus interest out of the proceeds. However, if you sell to buy another home the security can be transferred to the new home.

There is a similar Charge for legal advice and assistance. Any Charge will be modest because the amount of legal fees payable under the Legal Advice and Assistance scheme are small. However, it can mean that it is not worth getting legal advice and assistance to pursue a small matter like the return of personal possessions or money your partner has taken. You may be able to use the small claims procedure without legal advice and assistance. If the advice and assistance Charge would cause you grave hardship or distress your solicitor can ask the Board to waive it.

Appendix two

Going to a solicitor

Most solicitors in Scotland handle problems arising out of splitting up. You may already have a "family lawyer" who has acted for you before, but you may not want to consult him or her in connection with proceedings against your partner. Your friends may be able to recommend a solicitor.

How do I find a solicitor?

The local library may hold copies of the Legal Aid Solicitors Referral List or the Law Society of Scotland's Directory of General Services. These provide information on solicitors and what types of work they are prepared to handle. A solicitor can usually be found by looking for a Legal Aid sign displayed outside the office, or by consulting "solicitors" in the yellow pages. However, more accurate information on the choice of solicitor available can be obtained by consulting a Citizens Advice Bureau, which will carry information on what types of work local solicitors are prepared to undertake and whether or not they handle legal aid work.

Making contact

It is advisable to call or telephone the solicitor's office beforehand and ask for an appointment to see him or her, explaining briefly what your problem is about. All relevant papers should be taken to the first meeting with the solicitor.

Paying for a solicitor

Unless you qualify for assistance under the various legal aid schemes (see Appendix 1) you will be sent a bill in due course for the advice or action taken by the solicitor on your behalf. It is advisable to enquire about the cost at an early stage. Do not hesitate to ask the solicitor at the first interview roughly how long the work is likely to take and how much it is likely to cost. You may even want to seek quotes from several firms before selecting a solicitor to act for you. If at any stage you want a clearer idea of how the work being done by the solicitor is progressing and what it is likely to cost, follow up verbal questions with a letter (keeping a copy).

Appendix three

The meaning of some legal terms you may come across

Access (This was the legal term until November 1996)
The right to see a child who is living with someone else.

Advocate
A person who pleads or conducts a case in court.

Affidavit
A document containing a sworn statement which can be used in evidence. This avoids a personal appearance in court.

Aliment
Money paid to a spouse or child for their support - maintenance. The Child Support Agency has now taken over the assessment of most child maintenance from the Scottish courts. It does not use the term aliment - so aliment may now be used to mean maintenance paid specifically to a spouse.

Bankrupt
Insolvent. A bankrupt's whole property is made over by the court to a trustee in order that the trustee may sell it to pay the bankrupt's debts.

Children's hearing/panel
A tribunal consisting of 3 lay people who decide how to deal with children who have committed offences or who are in need of care.

Child support
A term used for child maintenance assessed by the Child Support Agency

Child support appeals tribunal
A tribunal that hears appeals against the Child Support Agency

Contact order
A court order stating who is to have contact with a child.

Custody (This was the legal term until November 1996)
The right of an adult (usually a parent) to care for and control a child.

Decree
An order of a court.

Defender
The person who contests or defends a court action.

Defences
The document lodged in court in which the defender sets out the facts and arguments contesting the pursuer's claim.

Domicile
The country where the law considers a person's permanent residence to be, or with which the person has most connections.

Exclusion order
A court order suspending a person's right to occupy the family home.

Expenses
The fees, outlays and other sums payable by a person involved in court action to the solicitors, advocates, court officials and others concerned in the action.

Guardian
A guardian has full parental rights and responsibilities and acts as a child's parent.

Heritable property (heritage)
Non-moveable property, mainly land and buildings.

Initial writ
The document which sets out the pursuer's case in the sheriff court (except summary causes). Service of this on the defender starts the proceedings.

Interdict
A court order prohibiting a person from doing the act(s) specified in the order.

Interim order
An order pronounced by a court pending final disposal of the case. Thus interim interdict, interim exclusion order and so on.

Legal rights
Rights of inheritance which can be claimed by a husband, wife or children even where there is a will.

Maintenance
A popular term used to refer to aliment and periodical allowance.

Moveable property (moveables)
Goods capable of being moved, money in cash or in accounts and "paper rights" like shares and insurance policies.

Occupancy rights
The rights to live in, occupy and return to a home.

Parental responsibilities and rights
The rights and responsibilities of an adult (usually a parent) to safeguard, provide direction and have a personal relationship and regular contact with a child. Until the child is 16 there is a responsibility and a right to act as a child's legal representative if required. The rights that an adult has are intended to be used to fulfil the responsibilities.

Periodical allowance
A weekly or monthly sum of money ordered by the court on granting divorce to be paid by one spouse to the other.

Proof
The hearing of evidence in a court action. Diet of proof - the date when evidence is to be heard.

Pursuer
The person who makes a claim in a court action.

Residence order

A court order stating who a child should live with. It can state that a child is to live for some time with one person and some time with another.

Sheriff officer

A person who serves documents and enforces orders of the sheriff court. The equivalent for the Court of Session is a messenger-at-arms.

Summons

The document which sets out the pursuer's case in the Court of Session or in summary causes in the sheriff court.

Will

A document in which a person states how his or her property is to be disposed of after death.

Appendix four

Books and leaflets you may find helpful

Divorce and Your Children, *Ann Hooper*, pub. Unwin.

Coping with Separation and Divorce, *Ann Mitchell*, pub. Chambers.

Bringing up Children on your own, *Liz McNeill Taylor*, pub. Fontana.

Learning to Live Without Violence - a Handbook for Men, *Daniel Sankin* and *Michael Durphy*, pub. Volcano Press.

Breaking up Without Falling Apart, *Ann Hall Dick* pub. Anna publications

Parents Apart, *Family Mediation Scotland*

Books for the children

I Have Two Homes, *Althea*, pub. Dinosaur.(Pre-school)

Dinosaurs Divorce,*L.K. & M. Brown*, pub, Collins (Primary school)

Me in my changing family, *Family Mediation Scotland*

Using a contact centre, *Family Mediation Scotland*

When Parents Split Up, *Ann Mitchell*, pub. Chambers.(10 - 15 year olds)

You Matter, *Scottish Office* (10 - 15 year olds)

Notes

Notes

Notes

Notes

Notes